Praise for

GREAT DAYS AHEAD

"Dr. Bowers has produced a gem of a self-help book. *"Great Days Ahead: Parenting Children Who Have ADHD with Hope and Confidence"* offers parents a rare combination of scientifically validated treatment advice delivered in a common sense commentary, infused with the wisdom of a father who has dealt with this issue on a very personal level. This book will prove to be an invaluable resource for parents of children with ADHD.

"The book is written in a clear, straightforward, useable style; parents likely will be unaware they are receiving knowledge and strategies based on state-of-the art research. Dr. Bowers incorporates anecdotes from raising his own children, stories from parents he treats in his practice, and excellent metaphors and analogies to bring his messages to life. The book is comprehensive in its coverage, including useful information on discipline, communicating with school, sibling problems, and peer relationships, to name a few. After reading this book, parents will come away with practical strategies they can implement immediately.

"I highly recommend that any parent who is struggling to raise a child with ADHD pick up this book and give it a read. They won't be disappointed."

– Michael Handwerk, Ph.D.
Licensed Psychologist, Harrisburg Medical Center (Illinois)

"After thirty years of working with parents, educators, and physicians, I have finally found a resource that captures the very personal and frequently overwhelming task of raising children with ADHD. *"Great Days Ahead: Parenting Children Who Have ADHD with Hope and Confidence"* provides parents with a well-paced, easy-to-understand journey that begins in early childhood and continues through adolescence. Through the vehicle of real-life challenges and emotions, Dr. Bowers and Dr. Borsh effectively teach parents sound principles of child development, learning, and behavior management. They emphasize the importance of co-parenting in the socialization and education of ADHD children, and provide excellent guidance on how to advocate for services within our schools.

"If I have learned two truths in my years of parenting, clinical research, and practice, they are, first, that children do not acquire understanding or skills from what we tell them. They learn by doing! Be it social, emotional, physical, or cognitive skills, children learn best by doing it over and over and over again. Second, it is clear that parents – not psychologists, counselors, coaches, and/or teachers – are most effective in creating opportunities to practice the skills of life that will maximize an ADHD child's chances for success. Dr. Bowers and Dr. Borsh have done an excellent job of empowering parents to do just that."

> – *George E. Williams, Ph.D.*
> *Licensed Child Psychologist*
> *Behavioral Pediatric & Family Therapy Program*
> *Lincoln, Nebraska*

GREAT DAYS
AHEAD

Also from Boys Town Press®

Common Sense Parenting® (Book and Audio Book)
Help! There's a Toddler in the House!
Common Sense Parenting® of Toddlers and Preschoolers
  (Book and Audio Book)
Good Night, Sweet Dreams, I Love You: Now Get into Bed
  and Go to Sleep!
Raising Children without Losing Your Voice or Your Mind (DVD)
Changing Children's Behavior by Changing the People, Places,
  and Activities in Their Lives
Common Sense Parenting® DVD Series:
  Building Relationships
  Teaching Self-Control
  Correcting Misbehavior
  Preventing Problem Behavior
  Teaching Kids to Make Good Decisions
  Helping Kids Succeed in School
Common Sense Parenting® Learn-at-Home Kit
Competing with Character
No Room for Bullies
Who's Raising Your Child?
Parenting to Build Character in Your Teen
Adolescence and Other Temporary Mental Disorders (DVD)
There Are No Simple Rules for Dating My Daughter!
Dealing with Your Kids' 7 Biggest Troubles
Practical Tools for Foster Parents
Fathers, Come Home

For Children

The WORST Day of My Life EVER!
  (Book and Audio Book)
I Just Don't Like the Sound of NO!
  (Book and Audio Book)
Visiting My Grandmother
My Trip to the Zoo
I Like Birthdays!
I Like Holidays!

For Teens

Boundaries: A Guide for Teens
Basic Social Skills for Youth
A Good Friend
Who's in the Mirror?
What's Right for Me?
Little Sisters, Listen Up!
Guys, Let's Keep It Real!

For a Boys Town Press® catalog, call **1-800-282-6657**
or visit our Web site: **boystownpress.org**

GREAT DAYS AHEAD

Parenting Children
Who Have ADHD
with Hope
and Confidence

Frank E. Bowers, Ph.D.
with Tara R.S. Borsh, Psy.D.

BOYS TOWN Press®

Boys Town, Nebraska

Great Days Ahead: Parenting Children Who Have ADHD
with Hope and Confidence

Published by Boys Town Press
14100 Crawford St.
Boys Town, NE 68010

Copyright © 2011, Father Flanagan's Boys' Home
ISBN 978-1-934490-14-3

Boys Town Press is the publishing division of
Boys Town, a national organization serving
children and families.

Publisher's Cataloging-in-Publication Data

Bowers, Frank E.

Great days ahead: parenting children who have ADHD with hope and
confidence / Frank E. Bowers ; with Tara R.S. Borsh. -- Boys Town, NE :
Boys Town Press, c2011.

p. ; cm.

ISBN: 978-1-934490-14-3
Includes index.

1. Attention-deficit hyperactivity disorder--Popular works.
2. Attention-deficit-disordered children--Behavior modification--Popular
works. 3. Child rearing--Popular works. I. Borsh, Tara R. S. II. Title.

RJ506.H9 B69 2011
618.92/8589--dc22   1107

10 9 8 7 6 5 4 3 2 1

Boys Town National Hotline
1-800-448-3000
A crisis, resource, and referral number for kids and parents.

This book is dedicated to my wife and life-long partner, Julie. Much of the art of parenting I learned from her, and her wisdom, patience, and gentle spirit have been goals to which I have aspired for over thirty years.

Acknowledgments

Parenting is an art first learned by being a recipient. As the recipient of good parenting, I am indebted to my parents, Ed and Lois Bowers. Thank you for your patience and guidance as I tested the limits during my growing-up years. Thank you also to my children, Jeremy, Nathaniel, and Shaun. You have all grown up to be fine men, and your daily commitment to great things has given me the confidence to write this book.

I would like to say thank you to my editor, Terry Hyland. Your patience, technical expertise, and guidance throughout this process have been invaluable. Without your encouragement, this book would still be an idea in my head.

I am professionally and personally indebted to Dr. Pat Friman. You have been my mentor, my encourager, and my guide for many years. Thank you for giving me the opportunity to work in a setting that makes a difference in families' lives. Thank you also for all of your words of personal encouragement to help me become a better human. Thank you also to my colleagues at Boys Town. Your commitment to excellence and zest for your work has made it fun to come to work every day.

Finally, I would like to thank all of the families that have let me into their lives. I especially want to thank the groups that allowed us to tape their sessions in order to gather information for this book. Privacy laws prevent me from acknowledging you by name, but please know how grateful I am that you were a part of my life.

– Dr. Frank Bowers

I would like to thank my family, friends, and most of all my colleagues at Boys Town for all their support throughout this writing process. I especially would like to thank my co-writer for being a mentor and motivator during my experience at Boys Town and while creating this book.

– Dr. Tara R.S. Borsh

Table of Contents

Speaking from Experience

I can't begin to tell you the frustration I felt when, yet again, I received a note from my son's teacher.

"Your son had a difficult time in school today...."

He was only in second grade and it seemed like every day was another "bad day at school." The same thoughts went through my head: "What is wrong with him?" "Why can't he just behave?" And the ever present, "What am I doing wrong?"

But then, you already know the frustration I was feeling. You are feeling it right now. That is why you picked up this book. You are looking for answers to those questions and many others.

I decided to go looking for answers, too. His teacher suggested that we have him tested for "ADD." I had never heard of that! So my wife and I found a specialist who completed the testing. Sure enough, our son was diagnosed with what was then called "Attention Deficit Disorder with Hyperactivity." This actually brought us a sense of relief. We finally had a name for "the enemy!" We now knew what we were fighting and this gave us some hope that we could overcome the difficulties.

Truthfully, the sense of relief was not only for my son. I now understood why I had been having difficulties with focus and concentration all of my life. The same behaviors we had been seeing in our son had been a part of my life for as long as I could remember. Now that my son was diagnosed with ADD, I suspected that I, too, could be facing the same challenge.

But I still didn't know exactly what ADD was. I knew our son was having difficulty with his behavior at school. And I knew he was not completing his homework. One night, he had an assignment to do ten math problems. I had him work at his desk in his room. Ninety minutes later, he had written his name at the top of the page and the numbers "1-2-3" down the left margin. Not much progress in an hour and a half!

The worst problem was that he was having a lot of trouble making friends. It was heartbreaking to see only one child come to his birthday party when he turned six.

In light of all this, I made a decision. Armed with a lot of questions, both about my son and myself, I went back to school to learn more about "the enemy." Three years later, I emerged with a Ph.D. in psychology, and with a little better understanding of what was happening and how I could help my son.

That was more than fifteen years ago. Since then, the name of the disorder has changed to "ADHD," and a lot more research has been conducted to give us a better understanding of it. New medications have come on the market and more effective interventions have been developed. My son is now twenty-six years old, and is doing well, thank you. I am proud of him for sticking with it and not giving up. It was not always easy, but armed with knowledge and a specific plan, we were able to keep "the enemy" at bay.

Over the years, I've met with scores of parents and children who struggled just like my family did. They were looking for answers, just like we were. Of course, not everyone has the luxury of being able to go back to school and make a major career change. But what those parents simply needed was someone to tell them how they could best help their child.

That's what this book is about. My colleague Tara Borsh and I have written it to help you by providing some hands-on, practical ideas for parenting a child with ADHD. The ideas and concepts in this book have been well-researched by professionals. I've not only taught them to my young patients and their parents, but I lived by them every day as my son was growing up.

Your child is precious. More than anything else, he or she deserves your love and care. We humbly hope the advice and guidance provided here brings your family closer together and helps you overcome the many challenges you and your child may be facing.

How's Your Parenting Toolbox?

There are a lot of tough jobs in this world. But none is tougher, or more important to the future of human beings, than the one we call "parenting."

Parenting is a responsibility you can take on with little or no formal training. There is no required "parenting degree" or a parenting license or permit a person has to apply for. Although you have to have a license to clean swimming pools, cut hair, poke earlobes, or do psychology, there are virtually no requirements for potentially the most demanding, all-encompassing, and important job of all – raising a child. In fact, most men and women become parents with only the experience of having been on the receiving end of the job; they were parented. For most of us, whatever else we learn about rearing a child comes from on-the-job training.

Like all jobs, parenting requires a certain variety of tools and the skills to use those tools. A carpenter would not consider trying to build a house if the only tool he had was a hammer. The more tools he is skillful at using, the more successful he will be at completing his task. Similarly, moms and dads should not expect to be successful at parenting if they learn and use only one tool. That's why it's so important to get as many good tools in your "parenting toolbox" as possible.

Successful parents have a variety of tools and understand how and when to use the right tool in a specific situation. And that's the real key to good parenting. You wouldn't use a sledgehammer to shape a diamond or use a jeweler's pick to dig for diamonds in a mine. Parents need to be able to identify and choose the right tool to accomplish a particular goal or purpose.

Your ultimate goal as a parent is to prepare your child to move out of the nest and be independent. You want to shepherd your child from birth to adulthood safely, with most bones intact, and to ensure he or she is emotionally, spiritually, physically, educationally, socially, and mentally prepared to take his or her place as a productive member of society. You also want to serve as a good role model for what a good parent is so your children can draw on those positive experiences if they decide to have children. This is a process, not an event. How and what you are teaching your child at any given time is a function of where you are and where your child is in his or her development.

This means understanding that a child is not just a small adult. Children see and think about the world in a much different way than adults. You are used to looking at adults in the eye. Kids look at adults in the kneecaps. Successful parents are ones who can understand their kids' perspectives and relate to them, communicating and instructing without giving up their authority as parents.

Employment coaches tell us that the best jobs are ones we would do and enjoy even if we weren't getting paid. Although parenting holds few financial rewards, successful parents love what they do and realize that how they raise their child will have a significant impact on the future of the world.

As difficult as parenting can be, having a child with ADHD makes this tough job even tougher. Since you are reading this book, you may have already experienced all the emotions that go with the territory – anger, sadness, frustration, exasperation, feeling overwhelmed, and many others. These emotions often have a way of unintentionally expressing themselves in negative ways when parents interact with their child. Before you find yourself at your wits' end and feel like you're losing all control, we hope using the tools we offer in this book will help you transform your home environment into one that is positive, loving, and productive.

This is a hands-on book. It will have done its job if it eventually becomes dog-eared, written on, bent, wrinkled, and well-worn. It's best to read this book in segments, rather than all the way through at once. There are stop signs throughout that will tell you when to put it down and practice the tools that have been discussed. As you become more skillful with each tool – not just thinking about it but actually using it – you will begin to see a difference in your child, and perhaps, in yourself.

The focus of this book is on parenting children who have either been diagnosed or are displaying the symptoms of

ADHD. However, these parenting tools can be successful with all children.

You are on a wonderful, exciting, and yes, sometimes frustrating, adventure. I hope this book helps you and your child reach your destination safe and sound.

CHAPTER 1

A Brief (and Helpful) History of ADHD

If you were to believe current popular media, you might think that ADHD is a current fad – the "illness du jour." Nothing could be further from the truth. The name has changed over the years, but the symptoms that we now call ADHD have been evident in children for many years. In order to better understand the disorder, and how the strategies discussed later in this book can help you deal with it, some background and history may be helpful.

The first known published description of the symptoms of what today is ADHD was written by Dr. Heinrich Hoffmann in 1844. Dr. Hoffmann was a German physician and writer whose sometimes-macabre humorous poems would describe various problems in children. One of his poems was "The Story of Fidgety Philip." The behaviors described in this poem may hit a little close to home for you – I know they did for me!

GREAT DAYS AHEAD

Let me see if Philip can

Be a little gentleman

Let me see, if he is able

To sit still for once at table:

Thus Papa bade Phil behave;

And Mamma look'd very grave.

But fidgety Phil,

He won't sit still;

He wriggles

And giggles,

And then, I declare

Swings backwards and forwards

And tilts up his chair,

Just like any rocking horse;

"Philip! I am getting cross!"

See the naughty restless child

Growing still more rude and wild.

Till his chair falls over quite.

Philip screams with all his might.

Catches at the cloth, but then

That makes matters worse again.

Down upon the ground they fall.

Glasses, plates, knives, forks and all.

How Mamma did fret and frown.

When she saw them tumbling down!

And Papa made such a face!

Philip is in sad disgrace.

Where is Philip, where is he?

Fairly cover'd up you see!

Cloth and all are lying on him;

He has pull'd down all upon him.

What a terrible to-do!

Dishes, glasses, snapt in two!

Here a knife, and there a fork!

Philip, this is cruel work.

Table all so bare, and ah!

Poor Papa, and poor Mamma

Look quite cross, and wonder how

They shall make their dinner now.

Now move forward several decades. In 1902, George Still, an English pediatrician, observed in his clinic the behaviors of forty-three children who were having difficulty with sustained attention. He also observed that these children were sometimes aggressive, mean, and dishonest. He called this cluster of symptoms "a morbid defect of moral control." Dr. Still theorized that these children's behaviors were caused by a medical condition and that their behavior was beyond their control. Additionally, he recognized a hereditary link to the disorder.

After an encephalitis epidemic in 1917, many of the children who survived the illness began displaying the same cluster of symptoms described more than a decade earlier by Dr. Still. This led to the name, "Post-Encephalitic Behavior Disorder." These children were observed to have difficulty with sustained attention and impulse control. Doctors theorized that the children's encephalitis had resulted in some type of damage to the brain. Once again, it was proposed that something organic caused these behaviors, and that it was not just a matter of a "bad kid" or "bad parenting."

In 1947, as soldiers were returning home from World War II, physicians began noticing that those who had sustained injuries to the brain had difficulty concentrating and were hyperactive. The similarity between these soldiers' behaviors and the behaviors displayed by children who had survived encephalitis further supported the idea that the behaviors in the children must have been caused by some unnoticed brain injury. This led to the name, "Minimal Brain Damage." However, as doctors continued to study the brain as well as the symptoms, it became apparent that these children, for the most part, did not have any brain damage! So the name changed again in 1960 – this time to "Minimal Brain Dysfunction." By 1968, the name had become "Hyperkinetic Reaction of Childhood." When the *Diagnostic and Statistic Manual, Third Edition* (DSM-III) was published in 1980, it contained diagnostic criteria for what was being called "Attention Deficit Disorder." During this time, the media discovered the disorder and the name "ADD" became a staple of our language. (The *Diagnostic and Statistic Manual,* which is now in its fourth edition, is the "bible" of behavioral and psychological disorders.)

The disorder's name would change one more time. When the DSM-III-R was published in 1987, the disorder was called "Attention Deficit Hyperactivity Disorder" or "ADHD." There still is some confusion about whether a child has "ADD" or "ADHD," but for diagnostic purposes, it is now all "ADHD." If this were not confusing enough, the DSM is scheduled to be revised again within the next few years. It is likely the name will change yet again when the newest version is published!

Why all the name changes? First, this disorder has been studied extensively for more than a century. In fact, it may be the most studied disorder in child psychology. As we develop a better understanding of the issues involved, the name occasionally changes to better reflect what we believe is actually happening. And since we still are not sure and are continuing to study the disorder, we will continue to refine the name. That's a good thing, because I would hate to think my son and I both suffer from a "morbid defect of moral control"!

What Is ADHD?

In practical terms, ADHD is a medical condition that negatively affects a person's ability to focus on required tasks and maintain attention. It also can cause a person to act impulsively, have difficulty sitting still, and feel like he or she is running at "full speed" all the time. Because it involves so many combinations of symptoms, it may look different in different people. It may also look different depending on the age and developmental level of the child. Symptoms that may be considered quite normal for a three-year-old could qualify as a diagnosis of ADHD for an eight-year-old.

If your child has ADHD (or if you suspect your child has ADHD), you've probably noticed several of the following behaviors:

- Difficulty completing tasks such as chores or homework

- Trouble sitting still, at the dinner table, for example

- Losing items such as one shoe, homework, or a pen or pencil

- Forgetting homework that should have been turned in last week because it's crumpled at the bottom of his backpack

- Being disorganized or messy (for example, having a bedroom that would be condemned by the Board of Health)

- Running ahead of everyone and maybe even getting lost in a store

- Talking incessantly

- Butting in on conversations

- Having difficulty waiting her turn

- Getting into fights over getting his way

- Flying down (or up) the stairs

- Not listening when you speak directly to her

These are just some of the behaviors that can frustrate parents. By the way, they also frustrate the child. Many

Living with ADHD

When my youngest son was born, my wife immediately stated, "There is something different about him." I have found over the years that parents often have a "feeling" very early that their child is having difficulty with attention and impulsivity.

When my son was four years old, our whole family went to the state fair. In order not to break the bank, we had a tradition that each of our children could choose one ride, play one game, and get one treat. (That still added up to a pretty hefty expense!) We stopped to get a treat for one of the older boys. When I looked around, my younger son had disappeared! Of course, panic set in. There were thousands of people around and we had no idea which way he had gone, if he had been abducted, or what had happened to him. I chose a direction and started running through the crowds, scanning left and right for my child. After a couple of minutes (what seemed like an eternity), I spotted him running behind the rides and hopping over the numerous electrical cables used to power the rides. In just a few moments, he had made it out of the midway and was trying to get to the ride he wanted to go on. He appeared oblivious to the danger he was in and had not yet realized he was "lost." Relief at finding him safe was soon replaced by frustration and a realization that I had to keep my eyes (and hands) on him constantly to prevent a recurrence. His impulsivity and hyperactivity (not to mention his speedy legs) meant that his mother and I would have to be ever vigilant – a task made ever more difficult by my own ADHD. X times, children with ADHD will make a statement like, "I am so stupid." What they really might be saying is, "I am so frustrated. Why do I keep doing things that get me in trouble? Why do the other kids laugh at me? Why is life so hard?" It really doesn't matter if their IQ is off the chart; they FEEL stupid, and no amount of persuasion or arguing with them will change that feeling. This frustration often causes children to shut down, leading to a downward spiral that puts them further and further behind, and further reinforces their feelings of frustration.

What ADHD Is NOT!

There is a lot of misinformation in the public media today about what ADHD is and what might cause it. If parenting treatments are designed around this misinformation, it often leads to a dead end, leaving children and parents exasperated and still searching for answers. In order to bring some clarity and accuracy to the situation, and give us all hope that we can manage our children's ADHD symptoms, it may be helpful to look at some of the myths surrounding ADHD that are currently out there and are often taken as fact.

Myth 1 – ADHD is the result of diet or food allergies.

In 1973, Dr. Ben Feingold theorized to the American Medical Association that there was a link between certain food additives and preservatives and the symptoms of ADHD. Although the popular media publicized this extensively and many parents worked very hard to control what their children were eating, to date, there has been no credible research evidence that children develop ADHD by eating these substances or that children with ADHD become more hyperactive from eating them. Also, restricting the sugar intake of your child, though probably beneficial for dental health and weight control, will probably not have much effect on her ability to focus and sit still.

Myth 2 – ADHD is willful disobedience.

Although it often may seem that your child is actively defying you, it is very possible that a distraction caused him to forget what you had asked or said. This does not excuse children's behavior; they are still responsible for how they act (a theme you will find repeated numerous times in this book). However, it is easier to focus on teaching your child when you maintain emotional control, and that is easier to do when you don't think of your child's behavior as a challenge to your authority. (Of course, sometimes we see ADHD and Oppositional Defiant Disorder occurring at the same time. In those situations, parents need to address both disorders.)

Myth 3 – ADHD is the result of poor parenting.

You may have heard people claim that all parents have to do is be stricter and quit "spoiling" a child by giving in to his behavior. People who say these things likely have never lived with a child with ADHD. Good parents who love their children and always have their best interests at heart know that no matter how many different strategies they've tried, from giving in to being very strict, their children still struggle with focus, concentration, and hyperactivity. Although appropriate parenting is critical to helping a child with ADHD (or any child) manage his difficulties, a lack of appropriate parenting is not the "cause" of ADHD.

Even with effective parenting, children's symptoms may not completely disappear and there may be areas where they continue to struggle. However, developing effective parenting skills and strategies for dealing with a child's ADHD will eventually help a child learn how to manage inattention, hyperactivity, and/or impulsivity in school, with friends, and with tasks. Most of all, these parenting skills can help you, as a parent, feel more in control and feel like you have a better way to address the problem behaviors that interfere with your child's functioning. These skills will give you hope that your child's symptoms will not always control your household and your family's life.

How Is ADHD Diagnosed?

The ways ADHD shows up in children are almost as numerous and varied as the children who have ADHD. With eighteen symptoms, there are myriads of symptom combinations that may present themselves. Each child is unique, and personality traits will interact with the symptoms in ways that will be unique. There are a minimum number of symptoms that must be present for a formal diagnosis, but what ADHD looks like with your child will likely be different from how it looks in other children. Although there are often similarities between children with ADHD, there also are many differences. The art of parenting a child with ADHD involves understanding the unique needs of your child and applying the best parenting tools available to meet those needs.

The symptoms of ADHD are divided into two groups. One group involves nine symptoms related to inattention. If a person has at least six symptoms from this group, he or she may be diagnosed with **ADHD, Primarily Inattentive Type**. This is what some people still call "ADD." The second group has six symptoms related to hyperactivity and three related to impulsivity. A minimum of six symptoms from the Hyperactive/Impulsive group may warrant a diagnosis of **ADHD, Primarily Hyperactive/Impulsive Type**. If a person has at least six symptoms from both groups, he or she is diagnosed with **ADHD, Combined Type**. In order to show that a child has any of these symptoms, they must be evident in at least two different settings, usually home and school.

So what happens if a child has only five of the symptoms of ADHD? Technically, this does not qualify for a diagnosis of ADHD. However, that does not mean the child does not need help. All of the strategies used to help a child with ADHD will also help a child who has some of the symptoms of ADHD, but not enough for a diagnosis. If your child is having difficulty with focus, concentration, organization, paying attention, etc., the strategies presented in this book can certainly help, whether or not a diagnosis of ADHD is made.

Unfortunately, ADHD is not an illness that can be identified or confirmed through a blood culture or urine sample. It is a behavioral diagnosis that requires the subjective assessment of experienced professionals. If your child is having difficulty with the symptoms I've discussed, you may initially want to talk with your pediatrician. Your pediatrician can guide you through the assessment and diagnosis process, which will likely include behavior rating scales for parents and teachers to complete. You also may be referred to a psychologist who specializes in ADHD for a more complete evaluation. Because there are numerous other issues that have the potential to produce ADHD-like symptoms, these issues must be ruled out as a cause for the symptoms before a diagnosis can be made. For example, a child who is not getting enough sleep at night may be hyperactive, have trouble with focus and concentration, and be irritable and noncompliant simply because he is tired. But his parents may think they're dealing with ADHD because the child's behaviors match the disorder's symptoms. If this child's sleep routine is improved, the symptoms may disappear. In this case, a diagnosis of ADHD would be a misdiagnosis.

How Is ADHD Treated?

In the 1930s, it was discovered that stimulant medications had a "calming" effect on children who were hyperactive and impulsive. Since that time, there has been an enormous interest in finding ways to manage the behaviors of children with these symptoms. Over the years, numerous studies have been published in many different journals, examining the effectiveness of various interventions for children and adults with ADHD. Most of these studies have examined the effects of various medications. However, a substantial number of reports also have examined the usefulness of other, nonmedication treatments. One of the largest, most comprehensive studies (MTA Group, 1999) suggests that a combination of medication and behavior therapy is the most effective treatment for children with ADHD.

If your child has been diagnosed with ADHD, it is likely that your physician will want to (or has) put the child on one of the medications used to treat the disorder. If this happens, your child's physician should monitor the effectiveness and side effects of the medication, and possibly increase or decrease the dosage until you are seeing the greatest benefits with the fewest side effects. In some instances, a child's medication may be changed due to side effects (e.g., irritability) or because he is not responding to the medication. Patience is the key here because it might take some time to find the right medication and the right dosage to produce the best results for your child.

Medications used to treat ADHD generally fall into three categories: stimulants, antidepressants, and antihypertensives. The most commonly used medications are stimulants. These include methylphenidate (Ritalin, Metadate, Concerta), amphetamines (Adderall, Dexedrine), and pemoline (Cylert). The vast majority of children with ADHD will be prescribed one of these medications. However, if a physician feels that one of these medications is not appropriate, an antidepressant such as Immipramine, Prozac, Zoloft, or Effexor may be prescribed. Another medication used occasionally is the antihypertensive, such as Clonodine or Guanfacine.

A nonstimulant medication, Atomoxotine (Strattera), has been approved by the FDA for use in children with ADHD. Since Atomoxotine is not a stimulant medication, there may be a lower chance of it being abused. However, unlike the stimulants, the initial therapeutic effects of Atomoxotine take some time to become evident (approximately two to six weeks). Additionally, several studies suggest that Atomoxotine is not as effective in reducing ADHD symptoms as the stimulant medications. Finally, the FDA has issued a couple of warnings, one regarding an increased potential for suicidal thoughts when a person first begins using Atomoxotine, and one stating that the medication should be discontinued if a child develops jaundice. Atomoxotine is usually not prescribed unless the other medications have been tried and have proven to be ineffective or produced unwanted side effects.

A growing concern in our society is the abuse of stimulant medication. Because stimulant medications can be misused, they have developed a street value. If your child is taking a medication for ADHD, it is important that you carefully monitor its administration. Don't just leave the bottle on the counter and remind your child to take the medicine. I recommend that you keep the medication in a secure place and give it to your child directly. You might also need to check to make sure the medication has been swallowed. Even though you might think your child would never abuse drugs, there is always the possibility that he could sell a morning's dose on the street for a good amount of money, and that temptation may be too strong to resist.

A mother came into my office recently and told me her seventeen-year-old daughter was on an ADHD medication. She was confident that her daughter was not abusing the drug, but was puzzled by why a thirty-day supply was not lasting the entire month. Her daughter was making excuses like, "I lost one, so I grabbed another one this morning" and "It's hard for me to stay focused in the afternoon, so I took a second one with me to school that I take after lunch." The truth was that she was "cheeking" the medication – holding the pill in the side of her mouth until her mother wasn't looking – and taking extras to sell at school.

One of the newest drugs to come on the market is called Vyvanse. Vyvanse is a pro-drug, which means it is a substance that remains inactive until it is digested. This mimics how the body creates useful chemicals and vitamins from our food. Because Vyvanse only acts as a stimulant once it is broken down by the stomach, a person cannot get high from grinding it up and snorting it, which is possible with other medications. This built-in safety feature makes it more difficult to abuse this drug (recreational use among young people is a growing concern), and more and more physicians are prescribing Vyvanse for their ADHD patients.

When it comes to using medication to treat ADHD in children, I have heard parents express concerns about "creating a drug-dependent child." They usually say something like this: "If my eight-year-old becomes dependent on taking a drug to feel better, won't he be more likely to abuse drugs when he's a teenager?" Actually, just the opposite is true. Children who are diagnosed with ADHD and get the proper treatment (medication and behavior therapy) are actually LESS likely to abuse drugs in adolescence than children who are diagnosed with ADHD and NOT given proper treatment. Perhaps this is because properly treated children have more control over their impulses, are not as peer-rejected, and have higher self-esteem.

In addition to medication, parents also must consider behavior therapy as another important part of treatment for their children. Medication is the key that unlocks the door, and behavior therapy teaches your child how to turn the handle and walk through. Behavior therapy addresses such issues as organizational skills, time management, prioritizing, communication skills, and pro-social skills. Behavior therapy also will likely include family therapy to address relationship issues between children and their parents, siblings, and peers. It is not easy living with a child with ADHD, and it is not easy for your child to have ADHD and live with you! Therapy addresses this issue and helps your family identify and effectively manage stress points.

If all the information in this section about medications, behavior therapy, and other treatment approaches regarding

ADHD seems like a lot to digest, that's because it is! Our intent here is not to overwhelm or confuse you, but to provide some terms and phrases you might hear as you and your child journey through the maze of diagnostic and treatment options. We hope that familiarizing yourself with this language can give you a head start and perhaps more insight into this disorder called ADHD, and help you ask the right questions and make the tough decisions you may face.

Congratulations!

You've made it through the first chapter of this book! I hope at this point you have a better understanding of what ADHD is, how it is diagnosed, and how it is usually treated. Now it is time to do a little exercise before moving on to the next chapter.

Go back to the list of behaviors on page 14. Look over the list and think about how many times (per day) you have responded to your child with some form of the instruction, "Stop doing that." Have you found yourself getting more and more frustrated every time you tell your child to stop? Have you found yourself using the word "Why" numerous times? By now, you probably already know that repeatedly telling your child to "stop" is not going to get the job done! In the next chapter, I will discuss different ways of parenting a child with ADHD. So take a deep breath as we explore more effective ways of changing children's behaviors without losing our patience and our cool.

Parents of children with ADHD

Parents of children with ADHD often feel overwhelmed, exasperated, and fearful that ADHD will prevent their child from being successful in life. If you have had these feelings, take heart. Over the years, many people who have made great contributions to society have exhibited symptoms of ADHD. Their "thinking-outside-the-box" approach to life has actually been an asset for them.

(During some of our most trying times with our son's ADHD, my wife would close her eyes and say, "I just know he's going to turn out great!" It helped us get through the daily challenges and, most importantly, she was right!)

Take a moment to look over the following list. One thing you will notice is that these people have been successful in many different areas of endeavor. Also know that there are many others with ADHD who have found success – they just didn't make it onto my list.

Here are a few famous people who were either diagnosed with ADHD or displayed the symptoms of ADHD: Ty Pennington, Bill Cosby, Jim Carrey, Robin Williams, Pablo Picasso, Whoopi Goldberg, Magic Johnson, Michael Jordan, Pete Rose, Babe Ruth, Albert Einstein, Benjamin Franklin, Leonardo da Vinci, Thomas Edison, John F. Kennedy, Prince Charles, Walt Disney, Andrew Carnegie, Malcolm Forbes, F.W. Woolworth, Samuel Clemens, Ralph Waldo Emerson, Michael Phelps, Justin Timberlake, Elvis Presley, George Bush (both of them), Tom Cruise, Charles Schwab, Nolan Ryan, and Buddy Rich.

CHAPTER 2

Seeing Beyond
the Problem

Let's do an exercise. Think back to the day you brought your new baby home from the hospital. See if you can recapture the excitement and joy from that day. Now think about the first time you heard your child say "Mama" or "Dada." Remember how proud you were? What about your baby's first step? Remember the excitement? These are just a few of the many treasured moments in the life of a developing child. Even during their worst moments, we treasure our children as a precious gift. And while you might be reading this book because you're frustrated with your child (or his or her ADHD) and need answers, you have to remember that parenting is one of the most rewarding "jobs" you'll ever have.

One thing I often hear parents say is, "I can't wait...."

- "I can't wait until she gets out of diapers!"
- "I can't wait until he gets bigger so we can play catch."

- "I can't wait until she starts school so I can help her study."
- "I can't wait until he's a teenager so he can get out and get a job."

Sometimes, we can get so focused on the "can't waits," we miss out on the wonderful "right nows" that are happening right in front of us. Why would we want to speed up our child's life when there are so many great experiences to share in the present? I can promise you that one day you will catch yourself saying, "I wish we could go back to when he was a baby, or a child, or a teenager…." What I have found is that each stage of a child's life has its highs and lows, its "A-ha" and its "Oh no!" moments, its joys and its challenges. Sure that newborn baby cries… A LOT! But at least she stays where you put her! And your toddler is now potty trained? Time to celebrate! Just make sure you keep your eyes on him because he's mobile now and can boldly go where he has never gone before! The good news is your sixteen-year-old just got his driver's license. The bad news is your sixteen-year-old just got his driver's license! If at each stage, all we see are the difficulties and negatives, we surely will miss all the fun and moments of elation our children can bring us.

This is an important point for every parent. But it's especially critical for those parents whose children have ADHD. We are so hypersensitive to the difficulties each day seems to bring that it's hard not to look forward to those "I can't wait" times when we hope and pray things will be better.

Here's the lesson: In every child with ADHD with whom I have worked, including my own, there have ALWAYS been positive events and proud moments, no matter what the child's age or how many difficulties a family faced. I know there are times as parents when we get so frustrated, so bogged down, and so focused on "fixing the problem" that we look right past the great things our kids are doing. It's like looking at the stars at night. They're beautiful, twinkling in the dark sky. But they're still right there during the day; you just can't see them in the sun's brightness. As parents, we have to make the commitment to not let the glare of our child's ADHD hide the starry beauty of his or her life!

Safe Passage

What is our main goal as parents? Most people would say making sure our children know they're loved and valued, and that they have everything they need to grow up healthy and happy. That's a good, and correct, answer.

But there's something even more basic we are charged with as parents. Our number one goal is actually to provide "safe passage" for our children. As I said in the Introduction, that means getting children from birth to adulthood with as few bumps, bruises, and broken bones as possible and ensuring they are fully prepared – physically, socially, psychologically, spiritually, educationally, and emotionally – to be productive members of society.

This is a challenge for any parent. For parents of a child with ADHD, it can be even more daunting. There's a greater need for patience and understanding. You have to learn to put aside feelings of embarrassment, frustration, and self-blame and put your energies into protecting your child. At the same time, you have to teach your child independence, confidence, and self-worth. There is always a tough balancing act between being overprotective and letting children do or have whatever they want.

Throughout this book, I encourage you to constantly think about the critical role you play as a parent in your child's life, how we learn to parent, and if having a child with ADHD has caused or forced you to change your parenting style. But above all, amid all the never-ending peaks and valleys of life, never forget what your goal is for your child – to get him or her safely to adulthood.

So where do parents of children with ADHD learn how to parent children with ADHD? Mostly through "OJT" – on-the-job training. We learn through experience and eventually develop a parenting style or approach that works best for our kids. But a few basics need to be in place for that to happen. If you were to write a job description for the position of "parent of a child with ADHD," it might read like the ad on the next page.

To better understand parenting a child with ADHD, let's look at some of the concepts that contribute to the different parenting approaches parents can adopt.

STOP

What other qualifications or requirements would you add to this job description?

HELP WANTED

JOB TITLE: Parent of a child with ADHD

JOB DESCRIPTION: Long-term, team players needed for challenging permanent work in an often-chaotic environment. Must possess excellent communication and organizational skills, and infinite **patience**.

HOURS: Must be willing to work varied hours, including evenings and weekends. Frequent twenty-four-hour on-call shifts. Some overnight travel required.

WAGES / COMPENSATION / FRINGE BENEFITS: None. But job has limitless opportunities for giving unconditional love, hugs, and kisses; watching a child grow; and feelings of elation for having overcome major hurdles. Daily positive emotions guaranteed.

RESPONSIBILITIES: Lifetime commitment. Must be willing to be hated, at least temporarily, until someone needs five dollars. Must be willing to bite tongue repeatedly. Also, must possess the physical stamina of a pack mule and be able to go from zero to sixty miles per hour in three seconds flat in case, this time, the screams from the backyard are from someone not just crying wolf. Must be willing to face stimulating technical challenges, such as small gadget repair, mysteriously sluggish toilets, and stuck zippers.

PREVIOUS EXPERIENCE: None required. All training is on the job, learn as you go.

BENEFITS: Rewarding but exhausting; satisfaction of knowing you guided a child successfully into adulthood.

Parental Support vs. Parental Control

There are important characteristics that make up the type of parent you are and continue to evolve into with your child with ADHD.

Consider the following two concepts:

- How are you providing parental support?

- How are you asserting parental control?

Parental support involves the amount of caring, closeness, and affection you provide for your child. Parental control is your degree of flexibility in enforcing rules and disciplining your child.

Graph 1

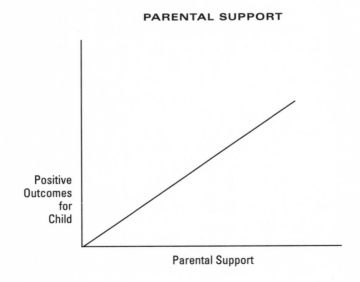

PARENTAL SUPPORT

Positive Outcomes for Child

Parental Support

As you can see in Graph 1, the amount of parental support provided is directly related to positive outcomes for a child. The more parental support you provide, the more positive outcomes result. Basically, you cannot love and encourage your child too much!

On the other hand, the positive outcomes of parental control are on a curve between being too lenient and being too strict. At those extremes, there is less of a chance that a child will experience positive outcomes. The best chance for good outcomes is somewhere in the middle of this curve, where parents are firm, fair, and flexible when enforcing rules and disciplining their children. These parents listen to their child and give consequences based on the child's specific behaviors.

Graph 2

PARENTAL CONTROL

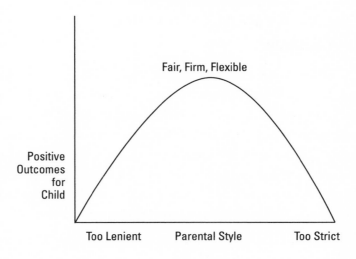

Parental control also should be based on the child's developmental level. In other words, a parent would use different levels of firmness with a five-year-old, a ten-year-old, and a sixteen-year-old. This is why it's important to know where your child is developmentally. (I'll discuss this in more detail later in the chapter.)

No matter what type of parent you want to be, it's important to remember that your child's ADHD will influence the type of parenting style you usually use.

In my work with parents of children with ADHD, I commonly see boys and girls who test limits, ignore parental instructions, and are disrespectful toward their parents. Early in therapy, many parents say they feel as though their child is in control of the home, and that they don't know how to get their parental authority back. This is often the result of parents misunderstanding parental control and parental support.

What Are We REALLY Teaching Our Children?

When you talk with or teach your child, he is learning much more than what you are saying. If you respond by getting upset when your child does not follow your instructions, you are teaching him how you prefer to handle frustration. The message to the child is this: "If things aren't going well, it is okay to respond by yelling, crying, or hitting." However, if you remain calm and neutral when your child does not follow instructions, you teach the lesson of staying calm and being patient.

Based on a parent's response, a child quickly learns how long he can disobey or misbehave before giving in and doing what's expected. The child is thinking, "When Mom counts to three, I can wait until she gets to two before I have to behave," or "I know Dad means business after he gives me my fifth warning," or "When Mom turns red and screams, I better run and do what she says." This is what we call *emotional parenting.* These parents are actually training their children how to test limits, or how far they can push a situation before they finally get a consequence. In the long run, these parents become frustrated, think with their emotions, and stop using logic or rational thinking when it comes to giving specific instructions, setting clear expectations, or delivering effective consequences.

On the other hand, a parent who expects compliance on the first command, gives no warnings, uses a neutral tone of voice, is consistent in giving consequences, and does not respond emotionally is a parent in control. We call this *purposeful parenting.* These parents send this message to their child: "I am serious and will not allow you to get me upset." They give a negative consequence when a child does not respond to their first instruction and they do not allow the child to control their emotions or behavior. Sometimes, it takes a while to reach that moment of clarity that sparks a parent's transformation into a purposeful parent. One mother told me her moment came as she finally realized that when she lost control and started yelling at her children, she was acting just like her fifteen-year-old daughter.

Have you ever been pulled over by a police officer for speeding? If so, how did the officer behave when he came up to your car window? Was he screaming at you and berating you for being a terrible driver? Probably not. He calmly asked you for your driver's license, insurance, and registration. He may have asked if you knew why he pulled you over. But he treated you with courtesy and respect. So why did you get those butterflies in your stomach when you saw the flashing lights in your mirror? Were you afraid he would hurt you? Or were you thinking, "Oh no, how embarrassing! I wonder how much this is going to cost me!" Had the officer approached in a huff and started screaming at you, you probably would have forgotten what you did wrong and started thinking about how badly he was treating you! You would have seen yourself as the victim rather than the guilty one. But the officer's calm demeanor and practiced manner didn't allow that to happen. You got a ticket and paid the fine (the consequence), and ever since, you've carefully checked your speed whenever you've driven down that stretch of road! That is the power of the ticket.

Your child thinks the same way. If you scream and yell at her, she can and will play the victim role and ignore what she did wrong. However, if you remain calm and simply take on the role of a police officer delivering a speeding ticket (the consequence you choose), your discipline will be much more effective. (More on this approach later.)

If strengthening the effectiveness of your consequences is not reason enough to convince you to remain calm, consider what you are modeling for your child. Don't you want her to learn how to handle stress appropriately? Aren't you trying to teach him appropriate conflict-resolution skills? Responding calmly to misbehavior with an appropriate, thought-out consequence will help your child learn these important life skills. Any child can struggle with learning and using social skills, and children with ADHD can have an even tougher time. Using every opportunity to appropriately teach and model these skills will pay dividends in improving your child's behavior in the long run.

To understand these concepts better, look at Graph 3 on this page. The "E-Line" on that graph is the emotional line. That is the "last straw," the point where, if a child pushes back too long or too hard against instructions or discipline, a parent loses emotional control and reacts with a consequence that may not only be inappropriate but also hurtful. This may allow the parent to drop back below the E-Line, emotionally and behaviorally, for a short period. But children by nature, and especially children with ADHD, will often try to push the parent back toward that E-Line. When parents allow this to happen because they are not consistently and calmly responding with firm discipline and appropriate consequences, families tend to constantly "live on the edge" of constant turmoil.

Graph 3

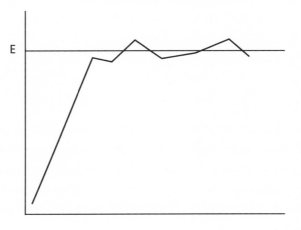

**EMOTIONAL PARENTING
VS.
PURPOSEFUL PARENTING**

Graph 4

EMOTIONAL PARENTING
VS.
PURPOSEFUL PARENTING

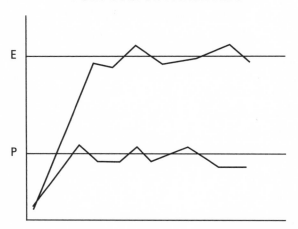

I recommend drawing another line, the "P-Line," which is much lower than the E-Line, as in Graph 4. "P" stands for purposeful, positive, powerful, proactive parenting. When a child pushes the parent past the P-Line, the parent delivers a pre-planned consequence immediately, which drops the parent back below the P-Line. The pattern is the same as with the E-Line, but the parent's level of emotion is much lower and keeps him or her from ever reaching that "last straw" situation.

There are several ideas to keep in mind when considering the P-Line, and I will discuss them throughout the book. I'll also refer back to the idea of purposeful parenting. For now, just understand that your goal is to stay at or below the P-Line and not allow your child's behavior to push to you toward the E-Line.

What Type of Parent Are You?

Imagine that you are in an extremely dark and foggy field. It's so foggy and dark that you can't see your hand in front of your face. You must get to the other side of the field. You cannot stay where you are. How do you feel about this? Many people feel anxious and nervous. Now what if I say there is a five hundred-foot cliff somewhere in the field? How do your feelings change? (When I use this exercise with parents, I've had several tell me that their anxiety level would jump and that they would be extremely cautious as they "crawled" across the field.) What if I said there is a fence ten feet away from the cliff that will prevent you from falling? I imagine that would make you feel less anxious and more confident about walking across that field. But I forgot to mention there are several large gaps in the fence. I'm guessing you've become more anxious again and will now use more caution when crossing the field.

Now imagine that the person walking accross the field is your child. The field represents your child growing up and trying to develop appropriate skills to pass safely into adulthood. The darkness suggests that the child does not know exactly where he is going or how to get there. The cliff represents all of the dangers, all of the problems, all of the things that you know can go wrong. Your child knows something uncertain or threatening is out there, but he may not know how to handle those situations. The fence represents you. You are telling your child, "Stay within these boundaries and you will be safe." The gaps in the fence represent any lack of consistency and persistency in your parenting. And there will be gaps. We cannot avoid them. We are human and we sometimes make mistakes. But we can minimize the frequency and size and scope of our inconsistencies by trying to make those gaps as small as possible.

How you help your child safely cross the field depends on your parenting style. The focus of this next section is on gaining a better understanding of why we parent the way we do.

Generally speaking, most parents learned what they know about parenting (fortunately or unfortunately) from how they were raised. You may view your parents as positive role models and respect their efforts in helping you grow up to be the person you are. You may seek their advice on parenting matters and want to emulate what they did so your children grow up to be respectable adults. Or, you may see your parents as negative role models and be frustrated that their voice or style continues to come out in the way you parent. No matter

STOP

Pause for a few moments and reflect on how you developed your parenting style. Have you spent time studying parenting or taken parenting classes? Do you have a consistent style of parenting or do you "fly by the seat of your pants"? Do you base your parenting style on "what is easiest" or do you embrace the difficult challenges that come with rearing children?

how you view your parents, one thing is certain: The way they raised you (and the way your spouse's parents raised him or her) influences the way you are raising your children.

Experts have identified four major styles of parenting. The first style is the *Balanced Parent*. These parents set clear rules and expectations, use good communication and consistent enforcement, and parent according to their child's developmental level throughout the childhood years. *Balanced Parents* see their role as providing nurturance and guidance. They focus on encouraging their child's positive behaviors while responding swiftly and firmly to negative behaviors. They use thoughtful and appropriate positive and negative consequences to shape their child's behavior, and deliver negative consequences consistently and immediately, not letting their child draw them into emotional battles. *Balanced Parents* have a strong fence (remember our dark, foggy field scenario?), with very few, very small gaps. They are flexible in their parenting style, being neither too lenient nor too strict. This allows children to freely explore while maintaining the safety and guidance they need to get to adulthood safely. The strategies and techniques discussed in this book are designed to help you become a *Balanced Parent*.

The second parenting style is the *My Way or the Highway Parent*. These parents have rigid rules, which they strictly enforce. Unlike the *Balanced Parent*, who also has rules, these parents leave no room for negotiating: Their child must do what they command or there will be hell to pay! They are on the "very strict" end of parenting styles. These parents rarely allow their children to think on their own. Children have little freedom or flexibility to explore who they are, show curiosity about their environment, or develop an opinion about their world. They are fenced in at one end of the field and held back from ever crossing it! The result may be a child (and later an adult) who is a passive follower who can be easily manipulated by peers. These children may allow others to think for them. Anytime a child challenges a *My Way or the Highway Parent*, he or she gets beaten up, emotionally, physically, and/or psychologically. So what happens with these children? Imagine your child turning eighteen or nineteen and entering the world alone, unable to think independently or make decisions without someone's help. How do think these individuals function in today's world? I will leave you with that thought as you ponder the effectiveness of this parenting style.

In my experience, the *Let's Just Be Friends Parent* is a common style of parenting today. These parents want their child to like them and would rather be their child's buddy than a parent. My response to that way of thinking is, "Your child already has friends. Children have opportunities to make friends but they do not have the opportunity to 'make' parents. You are their only opportunity to have a parent." Parents who practice this style will often give up their authority so the child will "like them" or "not be mad." These parents are on the "lenient" end of parenting styles. This opens the door for the child to take over as the controlling influence in the home. What that child wants, that child gets. The result is often a child who is spoiled, rebellious, domineering, and underachieving.

I'm not saying you can't be friendly with your children. Certainly you want to be kind and loving, and model for your child how to be friendly. But there's a difference between being a friend and being friendly. And you must constantly decide whether you are your child's friend or parent. If you are not a parent, then who's raising your child?

Children with ADHD often have difficulty making and keeping friends. Their impulsive behaviors and difficulty with identifying subtle social cues often alienates them from their peers. In this situation, a parent who has adopted this parenting style may feel emotionally responsible for meeting the child's friendship needs. But rather than trying to be a friend, it is more important for parents to focus on teaching friendship skills and providing opportunities such as play dates and sleepovers where a child can use those skills. (I will discuss this more in Chapter 6, "Fitting In and Finding Friends.")

Children will never tell their parents this, but they want structure. This is especially true for children with ADHD. With *Let's Just Be Friends Parents,* children may think they can climb over their parents' fence whenever they please. But deep inside, they want to feel safe and secure. They also may test the limits more often to see if their parents really mean it when they say "stay inside the fence." Permissive parents have weak fences that fall down easily when children push against them. The child who can do whatever she wants often becomes even more impulsive and aggressive.

The final style is the *Don't Interrupt My Life Parent.* These parents are more focused on themselves than on their child. They often think of their child as baggage and do and say things that make the child feel rejected and unwanted. These parents never even bother to put up a fence. They are too busy with their own lives to worry about whether their child crosses the field safely. These children often feel neglected, must fend for themselves, and sometimes will resort to extreme measures to gain attention and take care of themselves. Because they don't have parental guidance, they may come up with their own bizarre and irrational solutions to difficult problems, which ultimately will lead to confusion, frustration, and trouble.

It would be ridiculous to think that every parent fits neatly in to one of the four styles I've described. In real life, most parents have a combination of styles. But they may tend to lean toward or favor one style over the others. One way to identify your predominant style is to reflect on how you

Parenting Styles

Balanced: Parents have clear rules and expectations, which they consistently enforce. There is good communication between the parent and child.

My Way or the Highway: Parents have rigid rules, which they strictly enforce. The parents view themselves as the "supreme rulers" of the house and there is no room for negotiation or compromise. This often leads to conflict and estrangement between the parent and child.

Let's Just Be Friends: The parents turn over their authority to the child, whose preferences take priority. This can lead to rebellious, domineering, and underachieving children who exhibit more impulsive aggressive behaviors.

Don't Interrupt My Life: Parents are more focused on themselves than their children. Children often feel neglected and have to fend for themselves.

typically respond in a crisis or high stress parenting situation. Usually, your dominant parenting style will take over in this type of situation. It really comes down to learning how to adapt your parenting style to meet your child's learning and guidance needs, which are more challenging since you are raising a child with ADHD.

No matter what type of parent you are, remember that we all make mistakes from time to time (and that is okay). Parenting is not an easy job. There is no manual and there is no correct way to do something for every situation. If there was only one "right" way to parent, there would be no need for books like this.

Children are complex beings and the art of parenting involves discovering what works best for your child. This is especially true when you and your child are dealing with the symptoms of ADHD. The important thing is to have a clear understanding of your parenting philosophy and then make sure your techniques stay within it.

I think most of us often find ourselves thinking about how we were parented, especially in the middle of raising our own children. Children with ADHD challenge their parents every day, and I'm sure you have turned to the Internet, professionals, other parents, friends, and now this book to help you figure out how to encourage and shape your children's positive behaviors and decrease unwanted behaviors. You may even have said, "I will never be like my parents!" Guess what? Without even realizing it, you may be using the same parenting techniques and style your parents used. This is what you've learned and it may be the only set of tools in your parenting toolbox for dealing with your children's behaviors. Hopefully, what you're learning here will help you put more tools in that toolbox!

If it's time to mend your fences so your children can safely negotiate the dark, foggy field, there's no better time to start than now.

Modeling for Good Measure

Having a positive parenting style that focuses on teaching is important. But children also learn from the interactions they see between their parents and from the behaviors their parents model when interacting with others. Healthy interactions between Mom and Dad teach children how to solve conflicts and how to communicate with others.

Here's an example of what I mean: One night, Mom and Dad disagree on whether or not to go out for dinner. Junior observes his parents appropriately and calmly discussing the pros and cons of going out for dinner and agreeing on a decision together. Junior is learning that it's okay for people to have different opinions, and that they can express those opinions appropriately and use skills like negotiation and compromising to come to a positive solution.

By the way, with certain exceptions, it is okay to let your children see you and your spouse discuss, and even argue about, your difference of opinions. If a parent tells me, "We never argue in front of the children," it raises red flags. If it is true that this never happens (a highly suspect premise!), then they are setting their children up for unrealistic expectations in a relationship. A child begins to believe that "good" relationships don't have conflict and arguments. Then, when that child grows up and gets married, the first conflict he has with his spouse makes him question whether he is in a good relationship! It's inevitable that two people in a close relationship will have their differences and arguments. Modeling for your child how to appropriately handle those differences teaches him an invaluable lesson!

One exception I would make here is your discussions on how to parent and, in particular, discipline, your child. You and your spouse always need to be on the same page and present a united front to your child when it comes to parenting decisions. Sharing your differences of opinion on parenting with your child may open the door for her to take advantage of those differences, which can frustrate both of you. If you and your spouse differ on parenting philosophy, techniques, or goals, it is important that you discuss this privately and develop a plan you both can agree on.

Research indicates that happy couples tend to share child-rearing responsibilities, focus balanced amounts of attention on their relationship with each other and their relationship with their children, and agree on how to discipline their children. One of the greatest gifts you can give your child is modeling the caring, loving, cooperative relationship you have with your spouse. This teaches your child how to develop

STOP

Take a minute and think about what kind of behavior you've modeled for your child over the past week or two. Did your child try to use any of these behaviors, either appropriate or inappropriate, during that time?

healthy relationships with others and how to be part of a loving relationship, skills that are critical to the social development of children with ADHD.

Not every family may be able to do this. Single-parent families don't have the built-in mechanism to demonstrate appropriate interactions between adults. Nevertheless, single parents can model the components of a caring relationship to their children by the way they interact with significant others such as relatives and friends.

Where Is Your Child Developmentally?

One more critical factor to consider as you develop a positive, effective parenting style is your child's developmental level. Parents who know where their children are in their cognitive (thinking and language skills), emotional, and social development know how to set reasonable expectations for their behavior. Children who are able to change and improve their behavior because their parents set goals they are capable of achieving are more likely to find success at home, in school, and in their relationships with others.

Expecting a child to be able to do something that is beyond her developmental level is only setting that child up for failure. Can you imagine what would happen if a third-grade teacher decided to teach (and expected her students to learn) calculus? Students would fail every test and the teacher would be continually frustrated because the students weren't learning. That's why third-grade teachers teach fundamental, developmentally appropriate math skills and leave the calculus for a later time when children are ready and able to learn it.

Often, parents make the mistake of expecting their children to think like adults. But that's impossible because in children, the part of the brain that controls rational and reasonable thinking is not fully developed. You, as an adult, can think like a child but your child can't think like you.

Also, thinking is a complex process. For children with ADHD, it involves experiencing and sorting through many different emotions, feelings, personalities, rules, situations, and people every day, most of which can cause overstimulation. Even if these situations occur daily and are similar, children with ADHD often have to "start over" every day as they struggle to grasp, process, and respond to these factors. That's why they might frequently test your limits to figure out what walls they can break through and identify what rules will be enforced and when. Only through building positive relationships with others, seeing appropriate behaviors modeled, and receiving firm, consistent discipline can children begin to understand their world and make sense of what is happening around them. This is how they eventually learn how to express themselves in situations that are difficult for them, like being told "No."

Dr. Russell Barkley, a leading authority on ADHD, has suggested that children who are diagnosed with ADHD are approximately thirty percent behind their chronological age in socio-emotional development. For example, your ten-year-old child with ADHD has the physical body of a ten-year-old, but his emotional and social development may be closer to that of a seven-year-old! That might explain why children with ADHD prefer to play with younger children, act more immature than same-aged peers, and struggle to grasp social cues.

You are an adult. You act like an adult, reason like an adult, and (usually) feel like an adult. That is a good thing. You are showing "adult think." However, your child is NOT an adult! He is a child who acts like a child, reasons like a child, and (almost always) feels like a child. Your child shows "child think." It is not reasonable to expect your child to think or behave like an adult because he cannot.

Here's an example that illustrates what I'm saying: You tell your son not to do something, but he does it anyway. In your "adult think" mind, you reason, "I don't want him to do that. Maybe he didn't hear me. Maybe he just forgot. I don't want to have to punish him, so I will give him one more chance." You give him a warning: "Do what I ask or you'll get a consequence." In his "child think" mind, you son is thinking, "I don't have to do it yet because I will get another chance."

It is important to model "adult think" for your child with ADHD. But don't expect her to demonstrate it, at least until your child is an adult. For example, your child may want something based on her "child think" desire for pleasure and immediate gratification. She may even act impulsively to get what she wants. This is where your "adult think" of being

STOP

Think about the expectations you have for your child's behaviors? Do they fit his or her developmental level or are they too high or too low? What could you do to adjust them so they fit?

reasonable, rational, and goal-oriented kicks in to model for her the cause and effect, and possible consequences, of her actions.

Wrapping It Up

Parenting a child with ADHD presents endless responsibilities, challenges, and opportunities. At the end of the day, however, all of the little surprises your child brings to your life should make you feel rewarded and blessed. Regardless of where your child is developmentally, there are always positives that can be celebrated.

Remember that children always want our attention, and that it's our job to make sure we give it to them. Positive attention is better than negative attention, but in a child's mind, negative attention is better than no attention. Many children with ADHD need lots of attention. Because they don't always understand social rules, they may learn that the only way they can get attention is through using the kinds of negative behaviors that make parents want to pull out their hair. If we react emotionally to these behaviors, then children are getting something they want – our attention, even if it's negative. If we remain calm and deliver a logical, reasonable consequence, they will eventually learn that negative behaviors don't work and will begin using the more acceptable behaviors we should be teaching and modeling.

In this chapter, I looked at parenting styles, parenting support, and parenting control and how important it is for parents to model the appropriate behaviors they want their children to use. We also discussed the need to set reasonable expectations for a child's behavior based on his or her developmental level. In the next chapter, we'll look at the effect children with ADHD have on the family unit.

CHAPTER 3

It's All in the Family: The Impact of ADHD on Marriage, Siblings, and Social Situations

I could see the pain on her face as she sat across from me in my office. "I really do love my child," she told me, "but there are so many times I just don't LIKE him! Does that make me a bad mother?"

I understood the question. Children with ADHD often act in such impulsive and unpredictable ways that it is often hard to like being around them. However, the answer to that mom's question is a resounding "NO!" Feeling the way she felt about her son – or more specifically, her son's behaviors – does not make her, or any parent, a bad parent. It just makes us human. We have a natural desire to avoid unpleasant situations, even if they involve or are created by a child we love.

It is a sometimes a harsh reality that having a child with ADHD brings additional challenges, stress, and tension to the home, affecting everyone in the family. Think of a bird mobile that hangs over a baby's crib. If you hit one of the birds, all of the other birds begin to move, too. That's the way a family functions. What affects one person in the family influences everyone else. One person's emotions and behavior will influence the emotions and behaviors of other family members. Remember the E-Line graphs? A child with ADHD will often act so impulsively that a parent responds in a negative, emotional manner. But that does not make the parent a "bad parent." It just means the bird mobile is moving!

Here's an example: It's toward the end of a somewhat stressful day for a mother who's been taking care of her young daughter with ADHD and an infant son. Things have calmed down and the girl is momentarily occupied with picking up her toys. Dad walks in the door and the girl becomes distracted. She loses focus and begins running around the living room. Mom suddenly loses her patience and snaps, yelling at her daughter, "GO FINISH PICKING UP YOUR TOYS!" Dad, not thinking about the stressful day Mom has had, suggests that his wife be more patient. Mom then turns on Dad. "Don't you dare lecture me! You haven't been struggling with her all day!" Dad begins to get angry and yells back at Mom, "Quit yelling at me! I didn't do anything wrong!" Now Mom and Dad are arguing. The yelling wakes up the baby. The daughter starts crying. World War III erupts in the home. Why? It's really no one's fault. Just a bird mobile bouncing around. The bigger questions are how do we keep the mobile intact, protect our little birds, and make changes so everyone in the family is not constantly flying around in different directions? (Chapters 4 and 6 will also address these questions.)

As you begin to help your child improve his or her behaviors, the resulting changes will affect the feelings and behaviors of everyone else in the family. Hopefully, those feelings and behaviors also will change in a positive direction. Unfortunately, the impact is not always predictable. Randy was a fifteen-year-old diagnosed with ADHD and Oppositional Defiant Disorder. His mother brought him in for help with his behaviors at home and school. She was exasperated and frustrated with the upheaval Randy's ongoing behavior problems caused in the family. Johnny, Randy's younger brother, was just the opposite of Randy. The thirteen-year-old followed his parents' instructions, finished his homework on his own before bedtime every night, and was generally a joy to parent. Johnny received a lot of positive attention for his positive behaviors. Randy's behaviors drove Johnny crazy, so the brothers didn't spend much time with each other. After several therapy sessions, however, Randy's behavior began to improve. He was more compliant, got along better with his parents and teachers, and was completing his homework on time.

The bird known as Randy started bouncing in a positive way and began getting more attention. But as Randy received more attention, Johnny began to feel like he was not the "good child" any more. So Johnny changed his behavior (in the wrong direction!), acting out in an attempt to get back his "fair market share" of his parents' attention.

Although improvement in the behavior of a child with ADHD does not necessarily mean the behaviors of other children in the family will deteriorate, this story illustrates how everyone in the family (including you!) can be affected by any behavior change. As parents, it's important that you are aware of this and are prepared to address new, different, or unpredictable behaviors your other children might start using.

In this chapter, I'll touch on several key areas where a child's ADHD can have a profound effect on the stability (and sanity) of a family. Those include the marriage, sibling behavior, and social situations. I'll also provide some suggestions and tips on positive ways to deal with the problems that can arise in those areas. First, here's an exercise that can help identify factors that may be at work in a family with a child with ADHD.

STOP

Family dynamics are at play in every family. The list that follows includes some possible problem dynamics associated with ADHD family situations. Your assignment is to review the list and watch for them over the next week. Are any of them present in your family? If so, how are they influencing family relationships? Are they disrupting the safety and security of your family? How are you addressing these dynamics?

Enabling

This means making excuses for your child's negative behaviors and not holding the child accountable. This makes it easier for the child to repeat the unwanted behaviors. I've heard some parents say, "It is not my child's fault. He has ADHD!" But even though a child has ADHD, the window he "accidentally" shattered with a rock is still broken. And HE is responsible for breaking that window. A consistent mantra heard around my house when our kids were growing up was, "You are still responsible for your behaviors."

Excuse Making

Once enabling occurs, it sets the stage for everyone in the family to make excuses for the child's behaviors, including you.

Defensiveness

One family member feels like he or she is being blamed for everything. This makes everyone else the enemy.

Allying

Sometimes one family member will join forces with another for various reasons. This frustrates the person or people they are allied against. So if a dad and his son constantly team up to make decisions that go against what mom wants, it can create tension in the family and make mom feel left out and resentful.

Scapegoating

A child with ADHD is often blamed for all of the family's ills. Although his behaviors do influence the family dynamic, blaming him for all the stress in the home does not help reduce it and may lead the child to develop a poor self-image.

Enmeshment

Enmeshment means that people in the family don't have their own individual identities outside of the family. They are exclusively dependent upon each other. If one person tries to separate from an enmeshed family, that person is pressured to "get back into the fold." For example, in an enmeshed family, a child may have very few friends because her life is dominated by a parent's expectations and demands. The child might feel obligated to check with the parent on everything she does, from what she wears to who she dates. Even as an adult, the child may be compelled by a sense of "loyalty" to seek approval from the parent on decisions she must make.

Disengagement

This occurs when one or more family members separate themselves emotionally, psychologically, and/or physically from the other family members. When a parent disengages, this makes it much more difficult for the other parent to successfully parent the child with ADHD.

Overprotection

This usually means not allowing a child the space to explore and learn. Many times, parents of children with ADHD are overprotective because they don't want their child hurt by things like teasing or rejection. Overprotection means the parent is not recognizing the child's developmental level and is not helping or allowing the child to develop the life skills needed to be successful.

The Marriage

It is not uncommon for parents of a child with ADHD to have a strained relationship with each other. Oftentimes, one parent also struggles with the symptoms of ADHD, whether it has been diagnosed or not. I've often had a parent tell me in my office, "My son is just like his father. They are both so scatterbrained that I have to do the thinking for both of them." In these situations, parents with ADHD may develop feelings of guilt and blame themselves for their child's difficulties. On the other hand, the parent with ADHD may take the attitude, "There is nothing wrong with my child. I was just like him and I made it okay." In other words, these parents may be experiencing a mixture of relief, blame, guilt, or denial. This sometimes leads the other parent to feel that he or she must "parent" both the child and the spouse. This can really place an undue strain on the marriage relationship.

Feelings of resentment also may surface, with spouses asking each other questions like, "Why do I always have to be the one to (fill in the blank)?" or "Why are you always telling me what to do? You are NOT my mother!" These feelings may lead to arguments and fights. Each parent then may begin to withdraw emotionally from the relationship. The result is isolation, loneliness, and being overwhelmed by the task of parenting a child with ADHD with no perceived help from the spouse.

One of the biggest hindrances to a healthy relationship, whether it is with your spouse or your child, is the blame game. Much mental, emotional, and physical energy is spent trying to figure out who is at fault and who is to blame for the situation. The result often is defensiveness by the person who is being blamed and resentment from everyone else. When the issue is not resolved, feelings are hurt and relationships are strained. It doesn't really help the situation for the wife to remind her husband that he is forgetful, does not pay attention, or is impulsive. A better approach is to communicate with each other to come up with solutions to the problems.

Here are some tips on how you and your spouse can work together more closely to not only parent your child with ADHD but also strengthen your relationship with each other:

Remind yourself why you married your spouse. Those endearing qualities you found so attractive when you were dating are still there. They may be veiled by the daily frustrations of parenting and everyday life, but they are there just the same. If you focus only on the problems and bad times, you'll drown out the joys. Every time you feel like blaming or complaining to your spouse, recall a good time you've shared or something you love about him or her. Keeping your marriage strong is important for you and your kids.

Take time to discuss parenting strategies together so you're both on the same page. You and your spouse need to be in agreement on a parenting philosophy and a plan for putting it into action. This requires a constant discussion (outside the presence of the children) on your thoughts about parenting. Remember that whatever ideas you both have about parenting probably came from how you were parented. And because you were each raised differently, there may some disagreements on what you each believe is best for your children. The best approach is to lay everything out on the table and then work toward a middle ground where you both can be consistent in your parenting approach and strategies. It doesn't hurt to write down some guidelines that can serve as reminders for what you agree to do so your parenting can be consistent and effective.

Show at least as much (and preferably even more) patience with your spouse as you do with your children

and your co-workers. Remember that you're both in this together. Each partner has to give a little and show empathy for the other. Patience truly is a virtue when it comes to rearing a child. Being short with each other and constantly bickering won't accomplish your goals. Also remember that your children will grow up and move out of the house one day. Your spouse is your lifetime companion. Cultivating and nurturing a loving, healthy relationship not only will benefit your children but also prepare you for spending lots of time together during your empty-nest years!

Maintain a sense of humor. The fact that your child has ADHD is not funny. But being able to see the humorous side of whatever life throws at you is one way to get through the difficult moments. Everyone makes mistakes – including you! Sometimes, life's problems can be so daunting and so absurd, that all you can do is laugh. The ability to laugh at ourselves can relieve stress, help us relax, and give us a more positive view of what might at first appear to be an insurmountable challenge.

Work together as a team. In your quest to be good parents for your child with ADHD (and all of your children), there can be no sides. If you have begun to feel like you're on one side of the battle line and your spouse is on the other, it is time to work this problem out. Ignoring it will only make it grow bigger. If you and your spouse cannot work it out alone, seek professional help. A good marriage counselor who is familiar with the effects of ADHD on a marriage can guide you to a healthy resolution. Your whole family will be the winner!

Siblings

Remember the bird mobile above the baby's crib? When there's more than one child in the family, children with ADHD will affect the behaviors of siblings. The behaviors that annoy teachers and classmates – interrupting, blurting out, losing items, and others – also will annoy brothers and sisters, but to a much greater degree because they have to live with them every day.

I recently had a parent tell me, "Where the child (with ADHD) goes, so goes the family." What he was saying was that the emotions and behaviors of that child dictated the emotions and direction of the entire family. When siblings react to the child with ADHD with resistance or anger, parents have to deal with the fighting that results.

A family came into my office because of sibling fighting. Mom was tired of the older brother constantly yelling at and pushing around his younger brother. After a few questions, it became clear why this was happening. The two boys shared a room and the younger brother had been diagnosed with ADHD, Combined Type. Little brother often took big brother's things and didn't put them back; sometimes those things got broken or lost. Big brother was fed up and was using force to stop it. It also didn't help that the older brother was tidy; he liked his things put away neatly and wanted a well-kept room – an impossible standard for the younger brother. The result was resentment, frustration, and a constant battle between the two brothers.

I told Mom I thought each boy needed his own space, and that one of the goals of therapy would be to help younger brother learn boundaries and respect for others' property.

Although it wasn't possible for each brother to have his own room, the family reorganized their room to give each one his personal space. We then worked with younger brother on maintaining respectful boundaries and worked with older brother on how to handle frustration and get help when needed.

The biggest problem when siblings become frustrated with their brother's or sister's behavior is that they don't have the emotional tools or maturity to respond in a helpful way. That is why they resort to name-calling, put-downs, or even physical aggression to express their emotions. How can you restore peace in your house? Here are a few suggestions:

Although the "squeaky wheel gets the grease," it is important that you give all of your children attention, not just the child with ADHD. This means watching for opportunities with all your children to give praise when they behave appropriately. I sat in a school classroom one day to observe a child who had been diagnosed with ADHD. The parents were complaining about the child's behavior at home, but the teacher said she didn't have much trouble with him. What I saw was a masterful teacher using subtle skills to influence this child's behaviors. When the child would begin acting out, the teacher would walk close by without looking at or talking to him. She would then praise another nearby child for his appropriate behavior. When the disruptive child became quiet and returned to his task, the teacher then gave him her attention and praised him for his appropriate behaviors. I left there thinking parents can easily do this at home: Praise the child who is behaving appropriately and ignore the child who isn't. When the negative behavior stops or the child makes an attempt to stop the misbehavior, make sure you give him or her praise for appropriate behavior. The child will soon learn that positive behaviors earn positive attention and praise and negative behaviors don't.

Don't make your child with ADHD a scapegoat. You may be able to understand the frustrations of siblings, but always siding with them only alienates the child with ADHD. Help the siblings develop skills they can use anytime they are frustrated, not just when they are reacting to their brother or sister.

At the same time, make sure all children know they are responsible only for their own behavior, not that of others. The child with ADHD is responsible for his behavior. The other children are responsible for their behavior. Respond to each one individually, based on his or her behavior. A sibling should not be allowed to respond to his brother's behavior with physical aggression just because the brother has ADHD!

Look for opportunities to build self-esteem in the child with ADHD. When he's playing or otherwise getting along with his siblings, make sure you provide a lot of praise.

Social Situations

Having a child with ADHD can make you dread going outside the house.

For example, your family is planning to visit friends. But you have a knot in your stomach because you're worried that your child will misbehave when you are at their house. You talk to your child specifically about how you expect her to behave there, and when you arrive, just before you get out of the car, you say, "Now, remember, be on your best behavior." Inevitably, something happens. Your child accidentally breaks something, or gets in a fight with your friend's child, or gets into something she shouldn't be in. Or, you're taking a family road trip, a long-awaited vacation. You know the time in the car is going to be torturous. You try to plan many car activities to keep your child occupied during the trip. But you just know it is going to be stressful.

And what about your child's behavior in the grocery store? Do his tantrums embarrass you to the point of giving up? Does he run off while you are trying to decide which cut of meat is the best value? Do you spend a lot of time trying to find him?

If any of this sounds familiar, you probably wonder whether visiting your friends or going on vacation, or even going to the store, is worth the effort.

But it doesn't always have to be this way. With a little careful planning, you can map out the best way to navigate through social situations with your child with ADHD. By putting in some extra time on the front end to prepare your child, yourself, and the rest of the family for possible pitfalls and difficulties, you're more likely to enjoy a successful social experience.

Here are a few suggestions:

Practice appropriate behaviors with your child before going into social situations. You know how he has behaved in the past, so you can anticipate what problems might arise, and where and when they might happen. Just "hoping it doesn't happen again" will likely bring disappointment and frustration. Take some time to role-play the behaviors you expect your child to use. Practice a lot and be sure to give praise when he gets it right. Then reinforce those behaviors with praise when they occur in the real-life situation.

Give your child clear expectations she can understand. Carefully explain to the child why these expectations should be met and what the consequences will be if they aren't. Although you may have practiced the correct behavior beforehand, do not expect your child to remember everything you've taught. And don't expect her to get it right from the beginning. Children are not first-time, second-time, or even ten-time learners. They need lots of repetition and lots of practice. One mom told me that whenever she arrives at the store, she turns to her eight-year-old son before opening the car door and says, "Now, remember what we practiced at home. You are to stay with me and hold on to the shopping cart. If you ask me for anything, the answer will be 'No.' If you do not ask for anything and do what we've practiced, I may buy you something you like when we're all done shopping." Then, in the store, the mom involved her child in everything she did. He was not just a "tag-a-long"; she made him a "partner" in her shopping, talking, pointing things out to him, and asking him to put items in the cart. She said his behaviors gradually got better because he was active and involved, understood why good behavior was important, and didn't get bored.

Do not allow your child to hold you as an emotional hostage. I once observed a mother in a grocery store with a young child with ADHD. The child began to throw a temper tantrum when Mom told him he couldn't have some candy-like cereal. Mother calmly gripped the shopping cart and walked away, leaving the child screaming in the middle of the aisle. As soon as the mother turned the corner, the child quit crying, jumped up, and ran after her, yelling "Mommy, wait!" I went to the next aisle and watched as they walked toward me; the little guy was holding on to the shopping cart, and being very quiet. This mother, without saying a word, had told her child, "You are not going to emotionally blackmail me into giving you what you want." The child learned the lesson – at least for that moment. This is in sharp contrast to the parent who gives a child what she wants during a tantrum just to quiet her down and avoid embarrassment. Those kinds of situations should make any parent cringe. The lesson that child has learned is, "If I am obnoxious enough, I will get what I want." Not exactly what we want to teach!

Wrapping It Up

A child with ADHD brings numerous and varied challenges to a family. The effects of the child's behavior continually ripple through the family, influencing interactions and relationships between all members. As I demonstrated in our example, the bird mobile bounces – a lot. For parents and siblings, it often takes a lot of energy, patience, and thought just to make it through the day.

But there are ways to prevent and resolve much of the frustration, irritation, and anger families may experience. I've discussed some of those methods in this chapter, specifically in the areas of the marriage, siblings, and social situations. With greater awareness and a focus on consistency in your parenting for all your children, negative behaviors can be replaced by positive behaviors and the negative impact bad behavior has on the family can be reduced. As a parent, you must act with confidence and clarity as you identify and address the challenges your family faces.

In the next chapter and in Chapter 6, I will provide even more specific strategies for teaching children with ADHD the skills they need to succeed at home, at school, and in the community. By adding these effective tools to your parenting toolbox, you'll be setting your child, as well as yourself, up for success.

CHAPTER 4

Positive Strategies for Positive Results: Effective Ways to Discipline Your Child

A question I like to ask parents is "What is the end game of your parenting?"

Look at this way: Your family is like a business. You have raw material and you have eighteen or so years to turn that raw material into a finished product. We call that product an "adult." As I've said earlier, the goal of good parenting is to make sure your children, by the time they reach adulthood, are physically, psychologically, socially, emotionally, spiritually, and educationally prepared to be a productive member of our adult society.

If that is your goal (and I sincerely hope it is), then the next question is this: "Is what you are doing right now with your child moving you toward that goal or away from it?" In other words, is there quality control for your product and, if so, who's in charge of it? Parents commonly become so focused on the issue of the moment that they fail to see the bigger picture.

For example, a dad is so tired of his children arguing with each other in the house that he angrily yells, "SHUT UP!!!!" His immediate goal is to get the children to stop arguing, and he probably will succeed, at least for the moment. But the lesson he may be teaching his children is that getting mad and yelling is the way a person should handle frustration.

STOP

This is a good place to put the book down and reflect on and/or write down your goals for your child. What do you want your child to learn? What do you want him or her to take into adulthood? What and how are you teaching your child? As I discuss how children learn, take some time to think about how you intervene and/or give consequences in response to your child's behavior. What are these interactions currently teaching your child?

How We Learn

Many books have been written on the different ways people learn. Numerous theories are devoted to concepts such as the "visual learner," "experiential learner," "auditory learner," and "tactile learner." There is a lot of merit to those concepts. But when you boil it all down, there are really only two ways we learn – through **repetition** and through **contrast**. Try this simple exercise: How much is six times seven? Now, how much is eight times seven? I'm sure you answered "forty-two" and "fifty-six," respectively. But the real question is, how did you know that? You learned it through repetition. When you were in third grade, your teacher drilled math facts into your head over and over again, until you could answer thirty problems within one minute. So, repetition was required in order for you to learn math facts.

Now, how many times have you touched a hot stove – on purpose? Chances are, none, or at the most, once. So why did you have to repeat math facts numerous times to learn them, but only had to touch a hot stove once to learn to be careful around them? The answer is contrast. There is no contrast between the different multiplication facts. Those are just words that represent abstract concepts. But there is a great contrast between the temperature of your fingertip and the temperature of a hot stove. Or, more to the point, there is a great contrast between feeling fine and feeling pain! So, a good rule of thumb to keep in mind is:

The greater the contrast, the fewer the repetitions needed to learn a behavior.

Now, there are not a lot of experiences, like touching a hot stove, that will teach you a behavior after only one occurrence. Most behaviors require at least some repetition before you learn them. However, the more contrast you can create, the fewer repetitions will be needed.

What does this have to do with parenting? Well, let's say you need to put your daughter in time-out because she hit her little brother. Before you put her in time-out, she was playing by herself and you were busy with a task. Her brother took her toy, so she hit him. He started screaming, and you yelled, "Don't hit your brother! Go to time-out!" Your daughter goes and sits in your designated "time-out place" and you go back to your task. How is being in time-out any different from what she was doing before? She was by herself before, and she is by herself now! There is so very little contrast, it's likely to take an enormous number of trips to time-out (repetitions) before she learns not to hit her brother, if ever.

I will talk more about time-out later, but let's look at the same scene again, with a few twists. This time, instead of being busy with a task, you are interacting with your daughter. You are praising her for the nice way she is playing. She looks up at you and beams. You give her a pat on the back and tell her you love her. Moments later, her brother comes into the room and sticks his tongue out at her. She throws a toy at him and you sternly say to her, "No throwing toys. Time-out." She goes to where you point and sits down. Now, sitting in time-out, she isn't experiencing any of your attention, much less your praise. You totally ignore her repeated pleas of "Can I get up now?" She is experiencing a significant contrast between the good things that were happening when she was acting appropriately and receiving your attention and the isolation of time-out, where she is not receiving any of your attention. This contrast will likely reduce the number of repetitions needed to teach her not to throw toys at her brother.

Let's look at another example. I have asked many children, "How do you know when your mother is mad at you?" The vast majority of them will answer, "She yells at me." But I know a mother who trained herself to get quiet when she felt herself getting angry. I asked her children, "How do you know your mother is mad at you?" Their answer? "We can't hear her!" These children knew that if mom was speaking very softly, they better straighten up and listen, because someone was in trouble! One day, the children were playing in the front yard. Mom was on the porch watching them. The ball got away from the youngest and he started to chase it into the street. Mom saw a car coming down the road and, in her panic, yelled, "DON'T GO IN THE STREET!" The child, never having heard Mom yell before, stopped and turned to look at her. The car passed by and everyone was safe. The contrast was great enough to change the child's behavior in time to keep him safe. However, if that mom had been a "yeller," and the children had become so used to Mom's yelling that they paid no attention to it, her panicky scream may not have had the desired effect when the child headed for the street, with possible tragic results.

Keep the following concepts in mind as we look at different parenting tools:

1. **We learn through repetition and contrast.**

2. **The greater the contrast, the fewer the repetitions needed to learn a behavior.**

3. **Very few behaviors are learned with just one experience, making repeated opportunities to practice the new behavior necessary.**

Let's look at this third point for a few minutes. Think of how often you have heard (or said), "If I've told you once, I've told you a thousand times…." Sometimes, we assume that we only have to say something one time and our children's behavior will magically change. There may be a few children out there for whom that is true, but I have never met any of them. And a diagnosis of ADHD pretty much guarantees that numerous repetitions will be needed in order for a child to learn a behavior. Not to mention the fact that "telling" is a much less effective way of teaching a behavior than "providing an experience." (I'll revisit this later, too.) The take-away point here is that knowing it will take numerous repetitions to help your child with ADHD learn a new behavior should help you be more patient and encourage you to spend more time teaching and practicing new skills.

Here's another important point. I've often heard parents say, "I should be able to expect my child to do his homework every day without being told." Our answer to this statement is, "Yes! You should." But there is a difference between expectation and consistent performance. It is important to maintain your expectations – those are your goals for your child. But then you must teach your child, taking him from where he is now to where you want him to be. A child will not magically meet your expectations just because you have them. It takes modeling, training, practicing, and feedback to achieve that goal.

Just think of yourself as a coach who is having your player shoot one hundred free throws a day. A basketball coach expects his players to be able to hit a high percentage of their free throws. But his expectations do not translate into success without work. He first must model for the players how to shoot a free throw. Then he trains them on proper technique. Finally, he has them practice shooting numerous times, while giving them constructive feedback. As the player begins to hit more free throws, he begins to experience success, which leads to praise, which leads to more practice, which leads to more success, etc. Contrast this with a coach who just yells and screams at his players, without giving them the necessary training. These players experience failure, which leads to more yelling, which leads to less motivation to try, which leads to more failure, which leads to more yelling, etc.

You are the coach and your child is the player. You must decide what type of coach you want to be. Don't lower your expectations, but patiently coach your child to learn the behaviors you are expecting.

Giving Instructions Effectively

If your supervisor at work came to you and asked, "Would you like to help me out with a project?", you probably know your boss well enough to determine whether that statement was an invitation or an expectation. If you thought it was an invitation, you might respond, "No, I am really busy right now," and everyone would go on with life. However, if you knew it was an expectation, you would respond, "Sure, how can I help?" You, being an adult, have the capacity to understand the nuances or meanings behind questions or statements like these.

A child will likely have a more difficult time in similar situations. So, if you say to your child, "Would you like to put your shoes away now?", he may interpret your question as a choice. He could think, "No, I would not like to," and say so. But you weren't REALLY giving him a choice; you were setting an expectation for his behavior. When he says "No," you would take it as disobedience. So you punish him. But you're actually punishing him for being honest. And that is not teaching him what you want him to learn.

A more effective way to communicate an instruction is to make it a statement. There are three elements involved in giving effective instructions:

Get your child's attention. You cannot assume your child with ADHD will automatically tune in to your voice when you make a statement. In fact, just the opposite might happen; she may ignore you. Let's say you are in the kitchen and she is in the living room watching *SpongeBob SquarePants*. You call for her to come in and put her dishes in the sink. When she doesn't comply, you start getting frustrated. It is possible, even highly likely, that she did not hear you. Or, she may have been so focused on the TV that your words did not register in her mind. In order to give an effective instruction, I recommend that you start by looking at your child face-to-face and saying, "Iris (if that is your child's name), look at me." When Iris's eyes meet your eyes, you can assume you have her attention.

Make the statement. The important thing to note here is that it is a statement, not a question. It should end with a period or an exclamation point, NOT a question mark. Instructions that begin with the words "Could you…" or "Would you…" are not statements. They are questions that give options. And you may not like the option your child chooses! Some parents have argued, "But I want to be polite and teach them good manners." I agree. Let's teach them good manners. Feel free to add "please" to your statement. But just make sure your instruction is a statement. "You need to put your dishes in the sink, please" is just as polite as "Could you put your dishes in the sink, please?" And the expectation is much clearer. Listen to yourself the next time you give an instruction to your child. Are you asking or stating? Remember, a question gives options and your child may not choose the option you want.

Give a time frame. Many parents think the time frame is inherently part of the command. In their mind, saying, "Johnny, go put your shoes away" means "do it right now." However, children – especially those with ADHD – do not always pick up on this. It's better not to leave it to chance. For a child with ADHD, the only time frame that is appropriate is "right now."

You should say, "Johnny, look at me (get attention). Thank you for looking at me. You need to put your shoes away (make statement) right now, please (time frame)." Notice the thank you in the middle. Anytime your child follows an instruction (and "Look at me" is an instruction), you should give him praise.

STOP

Throughout the day, pay attention to how you give instructions and whether you are asking a question or giving an instruction or a command. Change your style if necessary, and focus on giving an instruction only once.

Why We Do What We Do

Have you ever asked your child, "Why do you keep doing that?" Typically, this is a cry of exasperation. You really do not want your child to respond with a fourteen-point thesis on why she continues to tell lies! You just want her to stop that unwanted behavior! Instead, the response you usually get from your child is something like, "I dunno!"

The truth is, there are only two reasons why anyone – you, me, and your child – does what they do. Although motivation for behavior can be dressed up and made to be really complicated, it is really pretty simple. We do what we do either to get something we want or to get out of something we don't want. Why do you go to work? To get something you want – a paycheck, a sense of accomplishment, socialization with your co-workers, among other things. You are driving down the highway, maybe a little faster than allowed by law, and you see a police cruiser up ahead. Immediately, you take your foot off the accelerator. Why did you do that? To get out of something you don't want – a speeding ticket! Even something as altruistic as volunteering or giving clothes to Goodwill is motivated by a desire to get something you want – if nothing but a good feeling or a tax write-off.

Your child's behavior is motivated in the same way. You put him in bed and he keeps popping up numerous times. What is the motivation for his behavior? Perhaps it's just to get out of having to go to bed! Or maybe he wants to play his video game some more. You may have seen a child in a store throwing a temper tantrum because his mother will not buy him that candy bar. What is the motivation for the temper tantrum? To get the candy bar, of course. So, if the mother gives him the candy bar (just to get him to be quiet so she will not be so embarrassed), then his behavior got him what he wanted. Which means, of course, that the next time he wants that candy bar, he will be even more willing to throw the tantrum!

Here is the key – give your child what he wants when he is giving you the behavior you want. Do not give him what he wants (or take away what he does not want) when he is giving you the behaviors you do not want.

In order to make this work, you must have a good understanding of what your child REALLY wants and does not want, not just what you think he wants. I had a dad ask me what I thought was wrong with his child. The conversation went like this:

DAD: I think my child is brain damaged!

ME: Why do you say that?

DAD: Every time he curses, I spank him. You would think after fifty spankings, he would learn not to curse!

ME: You would think. Let me talk to him and see.

Dad leaves the room and his son comes in.

ME: Tell me about this spanking thing.

SON: Oh, that. That doesn't hurt anymore.

Then he said the thing that solved the mystery:

SON: At least when he spanks me, I know he knows I'm alive!

Dad thought his son did not want to be spanked, and would change his behavior in order to avoid a spanking. But it turned out that the only time Dad would give him any attention was when he was spanking him. Because the son craved his dad's attention so much, he continued to curse in order to get the attention, even if it was a spanking! So what Dad thought was a punishment was actually reinforcing the negative behavior! I suggested to Dad that he spend some quality time with his son when he was acting appropriately, and then immediately walk away without saying a word if he heard his son curse. Soon after that, Dad told me he was no longer hearing his son curse.

So what does a seven-year-old want the most? That is a good question, and the answer will vary from child to child. **But I have found over the years that something children crave most often is attention, particularly from their parents. They want you!** They want your eyes, your kind words, your time. Oftentimes, the reason a child acts out (the boy cursing at his father) is to get some "face time." Certainly, there are other things a child might want. The child who throws a tantrum in the store wants that candy bar. The boy who keeps popping out of bed wants to stay up later to finish his video game. But, overall, the strongest desire for a child is to have your attention.

Time-In/Time-Out

Many times, I have heard parents say, "I have tried time-out and it does not work." But when I dig deeper, I find that what they are doing is not really time-out! They may be putting the child in the "naughty chair" for five minutes, or making her sit on the bottom step of the stairway or on her bed. And they are very intent on making the child stay put for the duration of the "sentence." But in terms of getting the desired results, it's usually not the real thing.

"Time-out" is really a shorthand way of saying "Time-out from positive attention or reinforcement." In other words, time-out is a state of being where the person in time-out does not get anything. Let me repeat that: NOT ANYTHING! So, what do you do if your child in time-out says, "Mommy, can I get up now?" If you do or say anything, your child is no longer in time-out because she got something from you – a response.

When a child is in time-out, he will do whatever it takes to get your attention. In a child's thinking, positive attention is better than negative attention, but negative attention is better than no attention at all. If you provide attention, then your child is getting the desired outcome for his behavior. In other words, the child's behavior is being reinforced. And if the behavior is reinforced, then you can pretty much expect to see it again!

Another reason time-out may not be working as well as you would like involves the way we learn, which I discussed earlier. Remember the rule? **The greater the contrast, the fewer the repetitions needed to learn a behavior.** Oftentimes, there is very little, if any, contrast between when a child is in time-out and not in time-out. In order to increase the contrast, two actions are necessary: Provide more attention when your child is not in time-out, and provide as little attention as possible (preferably none) when he is in time-out.

Because contrast is so important (and because it is just good parenting), I recommend that you look for and act on every opportunity to provide positive attention to your child. As Dr. Ed Christophersen, Chief of Behavioral Sciences at

Children's Mercy Hospital in Kansas City, says, "Catch them being good!" This is called **"time-in,"** which creates the contrast from the time-out you will provide when your child misbehaves.

There are three types of time-in.

- **Physical** time-in involves touching. It can be a "high five," a "fist bump," a hug, or a pat on the back. Any touch that communicates the message, "You did well," is a physical time-in.

- **Verbal** time-in involves spoken praise. "Good job," "I like the way you listened," and "Thank you for following instructions" are all forms of verbal time-in.

- **Visual** time-in involves eye contact. It could also include a smile, a wink, or other pleasant facial expressions, but mainly it is eye contact.

It is important that you provide as much time-in as possible every day. The more time-in you give a child for appropriate behavior, the more effective your time-outs will be.

Inserting or increasing time-in in a child's life can sometimes be the major environmental change needed to help re-direct a child's behavior for the better. Usually, though, a combination of time-in and time-out is necessary.

Remember, time-out is not a place. It is simply the absence of time-in. Here are some thoughts to keep in mind as you use time-out with your child.

Teach your child how time-out will work before you ever use it. This helps children understand what time-out is, why you are using it, and what they are supposed to do when it occurs. Teaching your child the process beforehand should help things go more smoothly when you need to use time-out for real.

There are two reasons for putting your child in time-out. First, she directly disobeys an instruction. You say, "You need to put your toys away right now." A few moments later (maybe five seconds), you notice that she is totally ignoring your command. This is a great time for a time-out! Second, your child breaks an established family rule. If a family rule is "No running in the house," and you see her running down the hallway, you respond with, "No running in the house. Time-out."

Do NOT give warnings! If you give a warning to your child, you reduce the effectiveness of the time-out. I once heard an exasperated parent scream at her child, "Do you want to go to time-out?" I half-expected the child to look at Mom and say, "Well, of course I want to go to time-out! That is why I have been acting the way I have!" The hot stove does not give warnings. It just does what it does. If you use the unacceptable behavior of touching a hot burner on a stove, the stove does not say, "Touch me again and I will burn you." It is merely going to provide a consequence for your behavior. That is what time-out should do: Provide an immediate consequence for a negative behavior.

Name the offense, and then say "Time-out" while pointing to the place you want your child to serve the time-out. Expect your child to go to that place. If he does not immediately go there, physically guide him. This is physical touch, which a child could perceive as time-in, so use as little physical guidance as possible. But once you say "Time-out," you shouldn't talk to or make eye contact with the child until time-out is over.

Rather than using a "time-based" time-out – usually some variation of one minute for every year of age, with a maximum of five minutes – use a "contingency-based" time-out. Make completing the time-out contingent, or dependent, on the child meeting certain conditions. In other words, release the child from time-out when you see he has accepted the consequence and is sitting quietly. When I am teaching time-out to children, I tell them the only way they can get out of time-out is to have "quiet hands, quiet feet, and a quiet mouth." I tell them this before I ever actually use time-out, not when they are in it. Remember, talking to a child in time-out is giving that child attention, which is not really time-out. By consistently using time-out correctly, you teach children through experience how they can end it. Once the child gets quiet for a few moments, say, "You're quiet. You can get out of time-out now." (If the child refuses to get up, start a new time-out.)

Once time-out is over, have your child practice the appropriate and expected behavior you want to see instead of the misbehavior that earned the time-out. When the child demonstrates the appropriate behavior, provide lots of time-in! If you put your child in time-out because she directly disobeyed your instruction, then give the instruction again. If she complies, then give lots of time-in. If she doesn't, then back to time-out she goes.

If you put your child in time-out because he broke an established family rule (no running down the hall), have him practice following the rule. After he gets out of time-out, have him walk down the hall two or three times, praising him each time he does it properly. This positive practice will help him remember to walk, not run, down the hall and earn him lots of positive attention from you as a reward for the appropriate behavior.

In my experience, the age at which can you start using time-out with your child depends on two criteria: mobility and resistance. The child should be able to walk to the designated time-out spot. Most children are walking by eighteen months, so this condition is usually easily met. The resistance part is a little more difficult to define, but most parents will know what it is. When the child shows you obvious resistance to an instruction, then it's probably time to start using time-out. Many children are already trying to assert their wills at age two by responding to their parents' instructions with the word "No!" That makes them prime candidates for time-out. Remember, it is the experience of the time-out that shapes the behavior. Language skills are not a necessary requirement!

When is a child too old for time-out? Technically, never. The method you use for time-out when your child is six will be different from what you use when she is older. But the concept of time-out continues, even into adulthood. If you have ever given your spouse "the silent treatment" because you were upset with him or her, then you have used time-out. A hockey player who spends two minutes in the "penalty box" for high sticking is in time-out! Practically speaking, however, time-out begins to lose its effectiveness when a child's desire for parental attention decreases, usually around age ten. (Your

Time-Out in Action

Mom: Johnny, look at me.... Thank you for looking at me. Please pick up your cars and put them in the toy box right now.

Johnny: No, I'm playing with them.

Mom: Johnny, you disobeyed me. Go to time-out.

Mom points to a spot on the floor and Johnny goes to that spot.

Johnny: Mom, can I get up now?

Mom ignores him.

Johnny: Mom, why won't you answer me? You're so mean!

Mom continues to ignore him. After about a minute, Johnny gets quiet and, taking a deep breath, sits there waiting to be let out of time-out.

Mom: Okay, Johnny, you're quiet. You may get out of time-out. Now, you need to put your cars in the toy box right now.

Johnny: Okay.

Johnny begins picking up his cars and putting them in the toy box.

Mom: Good job, Johnny. Thank you for following instructions.

child's age and developmental level will usually determine what approach is most effective.) Remember the rule? **We do what we do to get what we want or to get out of something we don't want.** As children get older, there will be other things they will work harder to earn – freedom, a cell phone, computer time, time with friends, etc. When that happens, another form of "time-out" – doing chores – may be more effective. Chores are delivered via "job cards," and they will be described later in this chapter. (I'll also discuss their positive counterparts, "joy cards.")

STOP

If you are a parent who will be using time-out with your child, this is a good place to start using time-in. To make time-out most effective, you should give your child at least five time-ins (a combination of physical, verbal, or visual attention) for every one time you give a negative consequence like time-out. Watch closely to see how these time-ins affect your child's behaviors.

Earlier in this chapter, I said children learn through repetition and contrast. In order to create the greatest contrast possible, you should provide as many time-ins as you can every day. Set your goals high; shoot for a hundred a day. This means looking for and praising anything your child does that is not a negative behavior. Make it your goal to consistently acknowledge these positive behaviors.

Once your child knows firsthand what it's like to consistently and regularly receive positive attention for using positive behaviors, begin to role-play and practice with your child on what a time-out looks like and how he or she can end it. Once your child understands the process, then begin using time-outs and time-ins to create the contrast between your response to your child's negative behaviors and positive behaviors.

Your Attention Is Requested

Have you ever noticed that your child seems to be in greatest need of your time and attention when you are least able to provide it? Often, it's precisely when you're in the middle of an important phone call or task that the interruptions begin. That is because things become more valuable when we restrict access to them. The oil cartels use this principle to control the price of oil, reducing output in order to increase the oil's value by driving up prices. When you are on the phone, your child has restricted access to your attention. This makes it more valuable to him and he works harder (whining, arguing, constantly calling for you) to obtain it. This is true for all children, but the situation is even more difficult when your child has ADHD. The child with ADHD has basically two time frames – "Now!" and "Not now!" The concept of "wait till later" is a difficult one for these children to accept. They have trouble delaying their desires until their parents are more available.

In these situations, it is important to respond to your child with redirection and an instruction: "Sarah, you need to take your toys to the bedroom. I will come find you when I get off the phone." If Sarah responds appropriately, respond with time-in ("Thank you, Sarah."). If Sarah does not follow your instruction and continues to interrupt, then a time-out is necessary ("Sarah, you disobeyed me. Time-out."). Remember that Sarah is going to time-out for not following instructions, not for demanding your attention. By the way, if Sarah has to go to time-out, don't forget about her while you finish your phone call. And if she follows your instruction, make sure you praise her compliance when you're done on the phone.

Job Cards

Let's revisit a scenario we used in an earlier chapter. If you've ever gotten a speeding ticket, you remember seeing the flashing lights in your mirror and getting this knot in your stomach. Why? Were you afraid the officer was going to shoot you? Of course not. But you knew you had been caught misbehaving, and you were going to be punished.

When the officer approached your window and asked to see your driver's license, insurance, and registration, he spoke in a calm voice, showing courtesy and respect. He then wrote you a ticket for speeding, and concluded the conversation with an encouragement to practice appropriate behavior: "Drive safely."

So, what is the big deal about a speeding ticket? Besides some possible embarrassment, it costs you money! You spent a certain amount of time in your life working to earn that money, and now, because of a misbehavior, you have to give that money away. Using money as a medium of exchange, you are technically giving away that time you worked as punishment for your misdeed.

That is what a job card does. The equivalent of a time-out for older youth who misbehave, a job card requires them to give up some time in their life to work on a chore or task as a consequence. You are the police officer, and it is your job to give the "ticket" (job card) to your child. And you should do it in the manner of that police officer who gives speeding tickets – speak in a calm voice, show no anger, and conduct a firm, confident, courteous interaction.

Did you have to pay that speeding ticket you received? Technically, no. You always have choices. But if you decided to ignore the ticket, a warrant would have been issued for your arrest. The police officer wouldn't call you every day to nag you about paying your ticket. Your choice would be either to pay it or go to jail!

Likewise, your child does not have to do the chore on the job card. Again, there are always choices. But until he completes the job to your satisfaction, he is grounded. This puts him in charge of how long the grounding will last. If he does not want to be grounded, then he should do the job card chore immediately. But if he chooses not to do it, he remains grounded.

The grounding should be total. Until the job card is finished, your child is restricted from almost everything and must remain in his bedroom. What CAN a child do while holding an unfinished job card? He can go to school, do his homework, do his regular chores around the house, go to regular church activities, eat his meals with the family (no dessert), and sleep in his bed. That is all. If he is caught doing anything else, he earns another job card!

The key to success here is that you must be willing to stick to your position, no matter what the cost. Otherwise, job cards will not work. If your child knows he can continue to play video games even if he has a job card, then the job card is meaningless. Read the story of the sleepy football player on page 92 to see how far you must be willing to go to enforce these rules.

Setting up job cards as a consequence is pretty easy. To begin, get about twenty (or more) three-by-five-inch index cards. At the top of each card, write the name of a job you want done around the house. These jobs should be age appropriate (you wouldn't want a ten-year-old to pull a card for "Cleaning the Gutters") and should be ones your child doesn't do regularly or routinely. Some examples are "Wash the Windows," "Clean the Baseboards," "Clean the Return Air Vents," "Sweep Out the Garage," and "Clean Out the Car." Underneath the job title, write specific details that describe exactly what you expect your child to do to complete the job. The rule here is this: If it is on the job card, it must be done; if it is NOT on the job card, it is not a part of the job. Remember, be specific.

Then put all of the job cards in a "Job Jar." When your child misbehaves, simply grab the jar, tell him the inappropriate behavior that is earning a consequence, and have him take a job card (without looking). This way, everything is random and your child has no control over what job he gets.

Just like the police officer who gives a ticket, there is no need for you to nag your child to get the job done. Remember,

The Case of the Sleepy Football Player

I was counseling a single mother, a rather petite lady, whose son was a high school senior. He was the starting quarterback for his high school football team. But he had a lot of difficulty getting out of bed in the morning. His mother told him, "From now on, I will call you once. If you don't get out of bed, you will earn a job card."

One Friday morning, she called him and he did not get out of bed. She said, "You have earned a job card." He took a card, tossed it on his dresser, and left for school. That afternoon, he came home from school and began getting his uniform together for that night's big game. His mother watched him, then asked, "What are you doing?" He replied, "Getting ready for my game." She stated, "Nope, job card." He started protesting, "You can't keep me from going to the game. I'm the quarterback. They depend on me." She ignored his protests and walked away.

He got the job on the card completed as quickly as he could. "Mom, I'm finished with my job card," he said. "Okay, you can go to your game now," she replied. He was late getting to the field and his coach yelled at him, but he made it in time for the game.

Later, I asked the mom what she would have done if her son had ignored the job card and walked out of the house. She said, "I would have called his coach and told him that my son could not play. He would have supported me. After the game, I did explain to the coach why he was late, and the coach said if I had any more trouble, let him know and my boy would sit on the bench."

he technically does not have to do the job. But make sure he understands that he is grounded until the job is completed to your satisfaction. Once the job is done, take the card back and end the grounding. This is NOT the time to lecture your child about why he received a job card – he already knows that, just like you already knew why you got the speeding ticket! Once the consequence is completed, however, you should do some teaching to help him understand why his behavior was inappropriate and how to make better choices.

Troubleshooting for Job Cards

So what should you do if you tell your child to take a job card and he refuses to reach into the jar? First, don't argue with him or yell at him about not doing it. Simply reach in to the Job Jar and pull out TWO job cards! The first job card is a consequence for the original negative behavior. The second job card is for not following your instruction to pull out the first job card. Now he is grounded until he completes BOTH job cards.

Now let's say your daughter has taken a job card. She knows the rule – she is grounded until the job on the card is completed to your satisfaction. After a few minutes, she calls out, "Mom, I'm finished with the job card." You discover she has done a poor job (to put it mildly) of completing the assigned job. In this situation, I recommend that you praise her for what she did accomplish, point out what she failed to do or failed to do well, and then say, "Now don't call me again until the job is complete and done correctly." If, a few minutes later, she tells you again that she is finished, and the job still is not completely finished or is done incorrectly, simply let her know she's earned another job card. This provides another

Job Jar

Quick Reference Guidelines for Parents

1. During a neutral time, sit down with your child and develop a list of jobs that need to be done around the house (inside and outside) that are not part of his or her regular chores. Make sure your child can do these jobs (for example, cleaning the oven would not be an appropriate job for a ten-year-old).

2. On a three-by-five-inch index card, write the name of a job at the top and a specific description of the job underneath. Repeat for all the jobs on the list.

3. Put the cards in a large jar. Explain to your child that when he or she breaks a rule or misbehaves, you will name the misbehavior and give the instruction, "Go get a job card." The child then must take a job card out of the jar without first looking at what the card says.

4. Your child must do whatever job is on the card. Until the job is completed, the child is grounded. The grounding ends once the job is finished to your satisfaction. This gives the child control over how long the grounding lasts.

5. When the child is grounded, he or she is allowed ONLY to go to school and church, do assigned chores, fulfill regular responsibilities, follow family rules, and eat meals with the family. Otherwise, the child must remain in his or her bedroom.

6. While grounded, the child **CANNOT** watch TV, listen to the radio or an iPod, play CDs, talk on the telephone, go outside, play games, have friends over, go to a friend's house, or have snacks.

7. When telling your child to take a job card, don't use a loud or angry voice, or nag or criticize. Also, do NOT give any WARNINGS, such as "If you don't do what I ask, you will get a job card."

8. Once the job is completed and the card is returned to the jar, the child is no longer grounded. Do not lecture about why your child got a job card. Later, when emotions are under control, do some teaching with your child about why he or she should follow your instructions or behave a certain way.

consequence that should discourage your child from trying to "just get by" on the first job card.

Here's another situation: Your son has earned a job card. He goes into the living room, and you hear him turn on the TV. When you look in, he's lying on the couch, remote in hand, watching a football game. Be careful! Don't cross your E-Line! Simply grab the Job Jar, turn off the TV, and say, "You were watching TV when you should have been completing your job card. You've earned another job card."

These situations may raise the question, "How many job cards can my child have at any one time?" Our rule of thumb is no more than three or four. I had one parent who gave her son twelve job cards in one day! The boy was overwhelmed and he just shut down. He took the attitude, "I already have a life sentence; what's one more day tacked on to the end?" If you find yourself giving too many job cards, you might want to start focusing on improving a few behaviors that your child repeats a lot and really needs to work on. Give job cards only for those behaviors until you see improvement. Then begin adding other negative behaviors to your job card list. Remember, there are many ways to respond to a child's negative behavior. But the best way to stop or reduce it is by consistently using negative consequences (job cards) the child will eventually want to avoid and providing praise and rewards when the child chooses not to use the behavior.

Joy Cards

When children are young, parents can use time-in and time-out to help shape their behavior. When children get older, job cards begin taking the place of time-out. But what about time-in? It is important that you continue to provide time-in, no matter how old your child is. Youngsters, teens, and even adults all enjoy receiving compliments, praise, attention, and an occasional pat on the back! You also might want to add "joy cards."

Joy cards are the opposite of job cards, but they're used in a similar manner. Joy cards are an opportunity for you to tangibly reward and reinforce your child for using appropriate behavior. To create joy cards, write a specific reward or positive consequence on the top of individual index cards. Place the cards in a jar labeled "Joy Jar." When you catch your child being good and using appropriate behavior, respond by saying, "You did a nice job. You just earned a joy card!" Your child then

I was stopped at a red light one day and was startled when a police officer began tapping on my window. When I rolled my window down, he stated, "I want to thank you for wearing your seat belt." Then he handed me a sport water bottle. Apparently, he was monitoring drivers, giving tickets to those who were not wearing seatbelts, and giving sport bottles to those who were. I drove away from that intersection with a more positive feeling toward police officers, and a renewed commitment to always wear my seatbelt. If job cards are like speeding tickets, then joy cards are like sport bottles. Using joy cards and job cards magnifies the contrast between rewarding positive behavior and giving a negative consequence for misbehavior, thereby increasing children's opportunity to learn.

Joy Jar

Quick Reference Guidelines for Parents

1. During a neutral time, sit down with your child and develop a list of rewards he or she would enjoy receiving. These can include things like reading a book together, choosing a TV program for the evening, extra time on the computer or video game, staying up fifteen minutes later than usual, and having a friend over to play.

2. On a three-by-five-inch index card, write the name of a reward at the top and a specific description of what it involves underneath. Repeat for all the rewards on the list.

3. Put the cards in a large jar. Explain to your child that when he or she behaves well, follows the house rules, or does what you ask right away, you may give the instruction, "Go get a joy card." The child then can take a joy card out of the jar without first looking at what the card says. You also can praise your child for the behavior that earned the joy card.

4. Depending on what the reward is, you can let your child enjoy it right away or make plans to enjoy it later.

5. After the reward, your child should return the card to the jar.

draws a card from the jar and gets to enjoy the reward written on it. Some examples of joy cards might be "Choose the TV Show for the Night," "Stay Up 15 Minutes Extra," "15 Extra Minutes of Computer Time," or "Get Out of One Job Card."

One rule I have for joy cards is that the child cannot ask for one. If your child feels she deserves a joy card and asks for one, your answer should be, "No, you may not ask for joy cards. You have to earn them." However, you should always be looking for opportunities to give out a joy card.

Wrapping It Up

In this chapter, I discussed the fundamentals of understanding our children's behaviors and how they learn, strategies for dealing with negative behavior, and how we, as parents, may sometimes reinforce those frustrating behaviors our children repeat over and over. These concepts and strategies will help you become a more purposeful parent, one who stays calm, cool, and collected like the police officer who issues a ticket for speeding. They'll also help you avoid the traps that go along with being an emotionally frustrated parent, one who can easily be manipulated by a child who recognizes your weak points.

Purposeful parenting is necessary if children are to begin learning what self-discipline is and how they must be accountable for their behaviors. Through contrasts, like those created by time-in and time-out or joy cards and job cards, they will learn which behaviors get them the positive attention they so strongly want and which behaviors will get them negative consequences or no attention at all. As you use these tools consistently and appropriately, you are likely to see a dramatic decrease in those unwanted behaviors like temper tantrums and not following instructions and an increase in positive, acceptable, expected behaviors.

CHAPTER 5

A Learning Experience: Advocating for Your Child's Education

One area of your child's life that is affected perhaps more than any other by ADHD is the school experience. Indeed, many children are first identified as possibly having ADHD in school. Usually, a teacher who has seen many children and who has likely had children with ADHD in the classroom before will observe some behaviors that raise suspicions. That kicks off a process, either through the school or a private referral, that leads to testing and ultimately a diagnosis of ADHD.

When a student has ADHD, it is important that parents and teachers establish and maintain constant communication with each other regarding the child's behavior and progress. Your child should see a "team approach" that shows him that you and the teacher are working together and are usually on the same page when it comes to decisions of discipline, behavior management, and monitoring. If your child believes you and his teacher are at odds with each other, he may use that as an excuse or reason not to follow the teacher's instructions, which can lead to even more difficulties.

I recommend that parents show support for the teacher in front of the child, and discuss concerns they have in private, outside of the child's hearing. Remember that your child's teacher is the authority in the classroom. One of your main goals is to teach your child to respect authority – all authority. He will be more likely to respect your authority (and that of other adults, like teachers, police officers, or a boss) if he sees that you expect and require him to respect the authority of his teacher.

Having said that, you, as a parent, should have the strongest (and loudest) voice when it comes to advocating for your child's education and participating in decisions that affect its quality. Children who are diagnosed with ADHD and complete an assessment that identifies a learning disability have certain rights, and schools are required by law to make sure they receive the same quality education as children without any disabilities.

Oftentimes, parents of children with ADHD (and other disabilities) are not aware of their and their children's rights in a school setting. They often feel left out of the decisions regarding their children, or are confused and frustrated by the myriad rules and technical language of the educational process for students with disabilities. This chapter will outline the primary laws that pertain to students with ADHD and the process parents should follow to ensure their children receive fair treatment. Most importantly, we encourage parents to take an active role in working with schools so their children can receive a quality education and get the maximum benefit, academically and socially, from their school experiences.

The Laws

Parents frequently seek professional help to find ways to manage their child's ADHD symptoms at home and in school. My clinic sees hundreds of them every year. Many of these parents are not aware that because their child has a disability, the child has certain rights within the school setting. Occasionally, parents will say they're frustrated because they don't think the school is providing the support they feel they need. It is important to understand that teachers operate under certain guidelines and rules, and usually have your child's best interests at heart. Nevertheless, it is also important that you are aware of the federal and state laws pertaining to children with ADHD so that you can advocate for your child. The purpose of this section is to briefly explain some of these laws and services, and how to request them from a school or other educational entity. Keep in mind that many of these services are government based and can be accessed only if your child attends a public school (elementary, junior or senior high, state university).

There are two main laws you should be familiar with: the *Individuals with Disabilities Education ACT (IDEA)* and *Section 504 of the Rehabilitation Act of 1973*. Both laws were designed to ensure that students with disabilities receive equal access to education and school activities and to eliminate discrimination on the basis of disability. The most important thing to keep in mind is that both laws guarantee a **free and appropriate public education** (otherwise known as FAPE) to all children. These laws were meant to "level the playing field" by providing services that meet the individual needs of qualified students in the same way schools meet the needs of students who don't have a disability. In other words, they allow children with disabilities to learn in the "least-restrictive environment" possible while receiving the same-quality education as children without a disability.

Under *Section 504*, children qualify if they have a physical or mental impairment that **substantially limits** one or more major life activities, including learning and behavior. Many children who have been diagnosed with ADHD qualify because they have difficulties with learning, behavior, and peer relationships. As a parent of a child with ADHD, you can request reasonable accommodations for how learning takes place in a regular classroom and/or through supplementary services, special education, and related services.

If a *Section 504* plan is not enough to help a child succeed in an academic setting under the *IDEA* law, the school **must** provide services and accommodations that are **individualized** to his or her needs. This should automatically entitle any child who might have a disability to a comprehensive evaluation by a multidisciplinary team at **no cost** to the parents. (The school district should cover these costs.)

The *IDEA* law strives to grant equal access to children with disabilities, and provide additional special education and procedural safeguards. For example, if a school attempts to suspend your child for ten cumulative days for a behavior issue, you can request a **Manifestation Determination** to determine if a link exists between your child's disruptive behavior and the disability. Even if your child is suspended or expelled, the child is still entitled to special education services. As a parent, you also can request an impartial due process hearing, otherwise known as the "stay-put" provision. Exceptions to these safeguards include incidents where children bring weapons or drugs onto school grounds or are at risk for harming themselves or others.

If your child requires individual accommodations, an **Individualized Education Plan (IEP)** will be created based on the child's specific needs. A team of people (which includes you) who are involved in your child's education determine these needs. Our advice is don't be intimidated. Go into these meetings with questions and ideas on what you would like to see implemented. Ask for clarification if you don't understand something or if you do not agree with an accommodation. What may appear to be routine or logical to others in the

---

IDEA & Other Types of Special Education Services

- Individualized to meet the unique needs of students with disabilities

- Provide the least-restrictive learning environment

- May include individual or small group instruction

- May include curriculum or teaching modifications

- May include assistive technology

- May include transition services and other specialized services (Occupational Therapy, Speech Therapy, Physical Therapy)

- Provided through an Individualized Education Plan (IEP)

- Allows for increased parental participation and protection of students

---

meeting because they have been involved in so many IEPs may be confusing to you. Feel free to make suggestions and ask questions. After all, the team should be working together so your child can receive the best education possible.

Your child's IEP should be re-evaluated every year or whenever a change in placement occurs, including a grade change.

By now you may be asking, "Even if I know the laws, how do I get my child covered under *Section 504*?" First, even though your child may have been diagnosed with ADHD by a pediatrician or psychologist, a school often will want to assess the child. Only the school can determine if your child qualifies. Just having a diagnosis of ADHD is not enough; there must be evidence that its symptoms are disrupting a child's education, learning, behavior, peer relationships, etc.

Here are the steps you can take:

1. Submit a **written request** to the school's principal and/or superintendent informing them that your child has been diagnosed with ADHD and asking for an evaluation to determine if the disorder is having a significant impact on your child's learning or behavior.

2. Request a copy of your school district's policies and *Section 504*. The school may have another name for it, such as *Procedural Safeguards* or *Parental Rights*.

Every school district has written policies and procedures that cover the referral-to-placement process. Make sure you understand your district's policies and procedures and that you and school personnel are following them. This improves the cooperative effort to do what is best for your child.

Occasionally, parents will complain that their child's school is not following its own policies. If that happens to you, you have the right to file a complaint about the school. First, contact the school district that is responsible for implementing *Section 504* and present your concerns. If this does not achieve the desired results, you can file a formal complaint with the **Office of Civil Rights (OCR)** by contacting the nearest state or regional office or calling the **OCR Hotline at 1-800-421-3481.**

Now that you know the process for requesting appropriate services for your child at school, here is a checklist for staying organized:

- Stay informed about what's happening with your child at school.

- If your child has an IEP, make sure you understand it.

- Communicate with your child's teacher frequently, both through school notes and personal and telephone conversations. Be proactive but don't get defensive when you don't always hear what you'd like to hear.

- Get information, services, plans, etc. in writing.

- Keep up to date on your rights as a parent.

- Play an active role in preparing your child's IEP or *Section 504* Plan.

- Keep careful, complete records.

- Try to maintain a good working relationship with the school by getting to know and communicating with teachers and administrators.

- Be encouraging toward the school, your child, and yourself.

Wrapping It Up

When it comes to being involved in your child's education, the bottom line is that you are working with professionals who have a lot of experience with children who have educational difficulties, including ADHD. And they want the same thing you want: for your child to receive a good education.

It is important to get involved early and to be involved often with your child's school, teachers, and administrators. As your child makes progress and the school situation improves, there may be a tendency to relax a little bit and back off. This is a mistake. Continual, meaningful involvement in your child's education is the key to continued success. (Chapter 7 contains more specifics on how to help your child find success in school.)

Remember that you are your child's strongest advocate and supporter. When children see their parents fighting for their rights and caring about their education, it shows them they also should care. There is nothing more powerful in the life of a child who is struggling than a confident, positive role model. The process may seem overwhelming, but it is worth all the time and effort you put in to it. And your child will thank you for being there!

Additional Resources

- **National Institute of Mental Health (NIMH)**
  Website: www.nimh.nih.gov
  Public Inquiries: 301-443-4513
  E-mail: nimhinfo@nih.gov

- **Child and adolescent mental health information**
  Website: www.nimh.nih.gov/health/topics/child-and-adolescent-mental-health/index.shtml

- **Children and Adults with Attention Deficit/ Hyperactivity Disorder (CHADD)**
  Website: www.chadd.org
  Phone: 800-233-4050

- **Attention Deficit Disorder Association (ADDA)**
  Website: www.add.org

- **National Center for Learning Disabilities**
  Website: www.ncld.org
  Phone: 212-545-7510

- **National Resource Center on AD/HD**
  Website: www.help4adhd.org
  Phone: 800-233-4050

- **IDEA Partnership**
  Website: www.ideapartnership.org

- **U.S. Department of Education, Office of Special Education Programs**
  Website: http://idea.ed.gov/explore/home

CHAPTER 6

Helping Your Child
Fit In and Find Friends

As the teacher called for the children to line up to go out for recess, Steve jumped out of his seat and ran for the door. He wanted to be first in line. Maybe if he was the first one out to the playground, he could be the captain of one of the teams today. But running in the classroom and pushing through other children only earned Steve a trip back to his seat. Now he would be the last one out the door. By the time he got out to the playground, captains had been selected and they were already choosing sides. Steve started jumping up and down, yelling "Pick me! Pick me!" But the captains kept picking other children. Finally, there was only one child left. "You can have Steve," one captain said. "No, you get him. We had him last time," the other replied. Frustrated and angry that neither team wanted him, again, tears began to flow from Steve's eyes. "Don't be such a baby," admonished one of the captains.

One of the most common problems children with ADHD experience is peer rejection. The behaviors a child with

ADHD displays often make it difficult for him to make and keep friends. If your child has several friends you approve of, count yourself (and your child) blessed. If, however, you notice that he is not being invited to birthday parties, is spending most of his free time alone, and/or is frequently getting into fights at school, it's time to address the reasons he is being left out.

Peer rejection is one of the most frustrating problems a child with ADHD (and his or her parents) will face. It is heartbreaking to see any child being shunned by her classmates; it's indescribably worse when it's your child. What do you say when she tells you she was the only one in her class not invited to a classmate's birthday party?

But the problem goes deeper than just feeling bad. Peer rejection is a major factor for predicting adult adjustment and mental health. One study concluded that peer rejection in the third grade was a more powerful predictor of later psychiatric problems than any other predictor, including teacher ratings, test data, self-report data, and even the evaluations of mental health professionals. This does not necessarily mean that peer rejection causes mental health issues, only that there is a relationship between them.

Healthy peer relationships for children are just as crucial as grades when it comes to school success. The earlier a child's difficulties with peers are identified, the more successful intervention efforts may be. Parents can be proactive by maintaining ongoing communication with important people in their children's lives, such as teachers, counselors, coaches, after-school providers, and health care providers. It's also a good idea to get to know parents of your child's classmates and peers; a close connection with other parents can be helpful in getting your child acquainted with children with whom they can start and build positive relationships, and possibly friendships. Checking in on your child's progress outside the home also makes it easier to identify social skills you can teach, model, and practice with your child.

For children with ADHD, making and keeping friends appears to be especially problematic. Their impulsive behavior, difficulty taking turns, being a poor loser, and irritability eventually lead classmates to reject them. Their inability to pick up on subtle social cues often results in behaviors their classmates would rather avoid. In group play, children with ADHD are involved in more negative verbal interactions and show more physical aggression than children who don't have ADHD. The end result is a downward spiral of rejection and poor self-esteem.

When children are rejected by their peers (as children with ADHD often are), they also miss out on essential opportunities to practice pro-social skills. As with any skill, if there is no practice, there is no improvement.

When my children were younger, they played organized youth baseball. The particular league they were in had a mandatory participation rule. The rule said that every child on the team who was at the game got to play at least three outs in the field and have at least one turn at bat. Though the rule was intended to make sure every child got to play, the more competitive coaches would come up with strategies for the best time to put in their less-skillful players. These players would usually end up in right field for three outs, where they would rarely touch the ball. And they would often get their one "at bat" with the instructions, "Don't swing, just try to get a walk." Meanwhile, players with more experience and better skills would play the entire game, getting three or four turns at bat. It was not hard to see which children were getting more opportunities to develop their baseball skills and which ones were limited in their opportunities to improve.

It's the same with social skills. When a child is socially isolated, ignored, or rejected, that child has fewer chances to practice the skills that can enhance social acceptance. At the same time, the child's inability to appropriately use social skills continues to be one of the main reasons he or she IS shunned! What a Catch-22!

In baseball, the young player who does not have well-developed playing skills can turn the situation around. He can spend more time practicing and going to the batting cage until his skills improve. Then, when he has opportunities to play, he can perform well and begin to earn more playing time. In the socialization game, parents have to do the same thing when their children have underdeveloped social skills: Give them "batting cage" time! This means teaching social skills through reinforcement and modeling, and providing opportunities for the child to practice using those skills with coaching and feedback. As children become more skillful, they will experience more success in the game of life.

When you think about it, appropriate social interaction is a complex process requiring a person to perform multiple tasks while making continuous adjustments based on the responses of others and/or the environment. The person is required to anticipate the situation, pick up on the subtle social cues being given by others, demonstrate appropriate verbal and nonverbal behavior, "read" the social feedback provided by others, and adjust his behavior based upon that feedback. If a person has difficulty with any of these tasks – and children with ADHD usually have difficulty with ALL of them – he is going to have a hard time with social situations.

It is important at this point to distinguish between a **skill deficit** and a **performance deficit**. A young boy who has never had a baseball bat in his hand has a skill deficit. He does not know how to hold the bat, stand in the batter's box, watch the ball coming in, judge where and when to swing, take a step forward, turn at the hips, swing the bat, etc. If he is going to acquire this skill, he must be taught. A coach will do this. Once the boy has learned the skill of batting, he does not have a skill deficit. However, if you put him at the plate in the bottom of the ninth inning with two outs, you'll probably be heading for the car soon. Just because he knows the skill does not mean he can consistently and effectively use it when needed. Now he has a performance deficit. Repeatedly telling him and showing him how to bat (and getting frustrated with him) will not improve the skill. Once he has learned the skill, the only way to reduce or eliminate his performance deficit is to give him a lot of opportunities to practice using the skill.

Knowing the steps of a skill is the first step in improving social interactions. But a child still needs continuous repetition to develop the ability to perform all the tasks necessary for a positive social interaction. Practice doesn't make perfect, but practice does make it permanent. Once your child knows the steps of the skill, it is time to practice.

So what skills does a child need in order to be accepted by his peers? That is a hard question to answer because some skills may be more beneficial than others, depending upon

Skill Deficit versus Performance Deficit

While in college, I discovered that children with ADHD are often the most peer-rejected children in the classroom. To address how to improve their social acceptance rate, I did a study, using "pull-out groups" to teach these children pro-social skills. I began meeting with fourth- and fifth-grade boys who had been diagnosed with ADHD, and who were being socially rejected, in a group outside their classrooms once a week for one hour. During this hour, we used a "teaching, modeling, practice, and feedback" format to teach these students skills such as "responding to teasing," "joining a conversation," and "waiting your turn." We were rather successful in our training. Eventually, all of the children were able to recite the steps to each skill and were able, within the group, to accurately follow those steps in a role-play situation.

However, when the children were back in their classrooms or on the playground, they were not as successful with using their skills. We observed that when they attempted to use a pro-social skill, the other children still rejected them. This would lead the children with ADHD to revert back to their old ways of doing things. Although they had learned the skills, these children were not able to successfully use them when the situation called for it. At that point, they did not have a skill deficit, but they did have a performance deficit. And no amount of "re-teaching" the skill was going to change the situation.

Our conclusion from that study was that peer-rejected children (particularly those with ADHD) often have developed a reputation and other children do not quickly accept a change in their behavior. Much practice and persistence is needed before that reputation can be changed and acceptance can occur.

the particular peer culture. For example, I knew a boy who was accepted by his male friends because he could burp on command. Although burping is not necessarily a skill that would endear him to his teacher or his parents, the other boys in his class were entertained by it and accepted him in their group.

Fortunately, there are a few basic skills that can enhance peer acceptance across many peer cultures. These basic skills can be categorized into three areas – Skills at Home, Skills for School, and Skills with Peers. The skills sometimes overlap and all of the skills are useful in each area. For example, although listed under "Skills at Home," the skill of Following Instructions also is an important skill in the classroom. For obvious reasons, burping on command is not one of the basic skills!

Skills at Home

1. **Following Instructions**
    a. Look at the person.
    b. Say "Okay."
    c. Do the task right away.
    d. Check back.

2. **Accepting "No" for an Answer**
    a. Look at the person.
    b. Say "Okay."
    c. Stay calm and don't argue.
    d. Don't do it.

3. **Accepting Consequences**
    a. Look at the person.
    b. Say "Okay."
    c. Stay calm and don't argue.
    d. Follow any instructions given.

Skills for School

1. Following Rules

    a. Learn what rules apply to the situation.

    b. Adjust your behavior to follow the rules exactly.

    c. Do not "bend" the rules – even a little.

    d. If you have a question, ask an appropriate adult.

2. Ignoring Distractions

    a. Do not look at the people trying to distract you.

    b. Stay focused on your task.

    c. Do not respond to questions, teasing, or giggling.

    d. If it continues, report the behavior to the teacher.

3. Waiting Your Turn

    a. Sit or stand quietly.

    b. Keep your arms and legs still. No fidgeting.

    c. Do not whine or beg.

    d. Participate when it is your turn.

4. Being Prepared for Class

    a. Gather all books, papers, homework, and pens/pencils you will need.

    b. Be on time to class.

    c. Turn in assignments when directed by the teacher.

    d. Write down assignments to complete.

Skills with Peers

1. Joining in a Conversation
   a. Look at the people who are talking.
   b. Wait until no one else is talking.
   c. Make a short, appropriate comment.
   d. Use words that will not be offensive to others.
   e. Give others a chance to participate.

2. Disagreeing Appropriately
   a. Look at the person.
   b. Use a pleasant voice.
   c. Say "I understand how you feel."
   d. Tell why you feel differently.
   e. Calmly listen to the other person's response.

3. Responding to Teasing
   a. Stay calm.
   b. Ask the person to stop.
   c. Ignore continued teasing.
   d. Seek adult help if the teasing does not stop.

(Of course, these are just a few of the many skills children need to learn. You can find a more extensive listing of skills in the book, *"Teaching Social Skills to Youth"* by Tom Dowd and Jeff Tierney, published by the Boys Town Press.)

How do children learn to use appropriate social skills? The same way they learn any other skill – through repetition and contrast. And because a person cannot learn social skills in isolation, it is going to require purposefully setting up situations that will give your child the opportunity to practice.

Begin by identifying what skills your child does and does not have. Start with the list just discussed. Teach the skills that are missing from your child's social repertoire. Once you have taught the skill, provide plenty of opportunities for your child to practice the skill.

If you are not sure what skills your child is missing, observe her in situations and environments where she interacts with others, especially her peers. Watch your child in school or on the playground and compare her interactions with those of other children. These observations may help you to become more aware of what additional help your child needs, whether it be in monitoring behaviors, learning how to interrupt appropriately, learning how to join or contribute to a conversation appropriately, thinking about how others feel or think, or even maintaining personal space.

Once you have identified the skills your child needs to work on, take the initiative to involve him in as many peer activities as your schedule will allow. Enrolling him in structured activities such as sports or clubs will give him an opportunity to practice his social skills as well as have shared experiences with peers who have similar interests. Let other parents know that you are working on social skills and would like their help in observing areas where your child struggles (for example, sharing, give-and-take of conversation, taking turns, etc.). Remember, learning social skills will not just "happen" with a child who has ADHD. It will require teaching, planning, and scheduling. You will need to "take him to the batting cage" often.

Your home is a great place to practice social skills with your child. One way to practice is to invite one of your child's friends over and have them play together in a neutral area. Limit the first play date to an hour or an hour and a half. The goal for this initial meeting is to allow both children to walk away feeling good about their time together. After this interaction, you can talk to your child about what skills he used well and what skills still need some work. Then, continue to build on and improve these weak areas. The next play date also can be structured and monitored. Then you can gradually decrease supervision.

Watching favorite programs on television with your child is another way for you to observe how she interprets what is happening in the social situations portrayed. Programs like sitcoms, which tend to be fairly predictable and sequential, are perfect for questions like "What do you think is going to happen?"; "What do you think she is feeling right now?"; and "What will happen if the character follows through?" This is a good exercise for children who have difficulty processing language or nonverbal cues and who often misinterpret what they are hearing and seeing.

As part of your normal routine, you also can have "special time" together where you and your child do an activity you both enjoy. This gives you an opportunity to observe how he responds in different social situations. When you "catch" your child doing something socially "good," give him lots of praise. Be sure to make the praise very specific so your child understands why he is receiving the positive attention (for example, "I really liked it when you were able to wait your turn just then"). You also can demonstrate some "inner dialogue," which may not come easily or naturally for children with learning and attention difficulties. This means "thinking out loud" with your child and giving him a private verbal prompt to use in certain situations. For example, when you are playing a game with your child that requires taking turns, you can teach your child to tell himself, "Gee, it's hard for me to wait. But if I can, people won't get mad and I'll have a better time."

I recently had a ten-year-old boy with ADHD in my office. The game we were playing was not going his way and I was watching to see how he would handle it. I was anticipating that he would become frustrated and begin to cheat or get mad and quit playing. Instead, he took a deep breath, calmed himself down, and used self-talk to remain positive. I stopped the game long enough to praise him for his efforts. He eventually lost, but said, "If we play next time, I am going to try harder to win." Once again, I used the opportunity to praise him, this time for losing with honor, a skill that is usually pretty difficult for a child with ADHD.

Wrapping It Up

Helping your child overcome social difficulties is a challenging task. Although you may be hurting for him, make every effort to be positive and encouraging. Your goal should not be to make your child the most popular student in school or the neighborhood. Instead, you should realistically strive to increase his positive social contacts and to develop at least a few good, meaningful, and lasting friendships. With more opportunities to interact with others socially, your child will be able to use the skills he is learning in real-life situations. There will still be times when your child is left out or ignored. But have patience and always be supportive. Those occurrences should begin to decrease as he gains confidence in using his new skills and learns how to fit in with his peer culture, make new friends, and enjoy acceptance.

CHAPTER 7

But What About...?
Advice on Homework and
Other Daily Routines

So far, this book has presented many theories, concepts, and ideas about parenting children with ADHD and has discussed specific techniques and strategies that you can add to your parenting "toolbox." In this chapter, I'll provide some examples of how to apply these theories and techniques in specific parenting areas. The situations presented here are by no means exhaustive (though these situations can prove to be EXHAUSTING for parents of children with ADHD!). But they are some of the more common challenges I have encountered in our work with parents. Remember, your parenting tools can be used in almost any situation as long as you remain true to the principles of parenting.

Because these are parenting situations you are likely to deal with daily, they are presented in the order they might occur with your child over the course of a normal day. Let's start with morning routines.

Morning Routines

Does this sound familiar?

From the first of six times you have to call your child to get out of bed, until he enters the school building (finally!), your morning routine is filled with nagging, tension, and frustration. Not only are you running late because he was slow getting out of bed, but you continue to run later because it seems to take him forever to complete his morning tasks. (One mom asked me, "Should it really take him ten minutes just to pull a shirt over his head?") Then, he can't find his shoes. So he wanders around the house, "looking" for them. In the meantime, you become more and more frustrated. Finally, he is dressed, fed, and ready to get in the car. Maybe you will be able to get him to school on time today. But once you're in the car, he says, "Oh, Mom. I forgot. I need to bring a poster board to school today. Can we stop at the store on the way to school and get one?" Does this send you over your E-Line? By the time he finally gets out of the car at school, you are emotionally drained, again, and he stomps off to class, tired of your yelling!

Children with ADHD often have a more difficult time getting ready in the morning for several reasons. First, they get started late because they have a hard time waking up. That's because they probably had a difficult time going to sleep the night before. Then, they are easily distracted. So if the TV is on, they are likely to stop what they are doing to watch cartoons! Also, they often lose things that are necessary for their day. So they have to take extra time to hunt down what they cannot find.

Here are some suggestions to help make your mornings go more smoothly.

During your bedtime routine (discussed later in the chapter), do as much preparation for the following morning as possible. For example, have your child get his books together and put them all in his backpack. Then have him place his backpack by the front door before he goes to bed. That way, it will be right there for him in the morning. He also can lay out his clothes (and find that lost shoe) the night before.

Get your child an alarm clock and work with him on getting up when the alarm sounds. He should get into the routine of getting himself up without you having to call him. If he has trouble with this, don't call him. Instead, when you hear his alarm, dampen a wash cloth with cool water and walk toward his room. If he is not awake and up by the time you get to his bed, gently rub his face with the wet washcloth. (Don't say anything.) This will wake him up (possibly in a somewhat bad mood the first few times) and he will soon learn that by getting up to his alarm, he can avoid the wet washcloth.

Remember, your child is easily distracted. **Reduce the number of distractions,** especially by leaving the TV off in the morning. If he is completely ready before it's time to go, reward him by letting him watch a few minutes of TV until you leave. This may be an incentive for him to stay on task and get ready early, rather than rushing to finish everything at the last minute.

Make sure he knows what time his ride (whether it's with you or someone else) is leaving for school. Make sure it leaves at the scheduled time. Make sure he is in the vehicle when it leaves, even if he still doesn't have his shoes on. He can put them on during the ride.

If he continues to have difficulty, **set the alarm for an earlier wake-up** so he has more time to get ready. Of course, this means going to bed earlier so he gets the sleep he needs.

Sometimes it is helpful to **make a list of morning duties** and have him follow it. This will help him stay organized and on task, and will ensure he doesn't forget to do something important like brush his teeth.

Homework/Schoolwork

Academic success is one of the most elusive and frustrating areas for children with ADHD. In fact, difficulties a child is having at school often are the catalyst for having a child assessed for ADHD. There is no connection between intelligence and ADHD. Being diagnosed with ADHD does not mean a child is "slow" or "low functioning." However, children with ADHD usually struggle with staying on task, completing schoolwork and homework, being organized, staying focused, and getting work turned in on time, regardless of their ability. These difficulties often result in lower scores on tests, daily work, and report cards.

The following suggestions can be helpful as you work with your child to be successful in school.

To increase your child's opportunities for success, help him establish study routines and habits. It is a mistake to let a child with ADHD rely solely on his memory. Remembering to do something that is important can easily get lost in other thoughts and the task never gets done. By following routines and habits, a child has fewer tasks and behaviors to trust to memory. For example, how many times has your child arrived at school only to discover that the homework he struggled with the night before is not in his backpack? By getting into the habit of always putting completed homework in a homework folder and putting the folder in the backpack, there's a better chance the homework will be there when your child needs it.

Use home-school notes to improve communication with your child's teacher and keep track of schoolwork. I'm sure your child has often told you, "I don't have any homework," and you found out later she is missing numerous assignments. Usually, it's not a case of your child lying to you because she didn't want to do her homework. More often than not, she simply forgot she had any! A solution for this is the home-school note. The home-school note is a way for you and your child's teachers to communicate that makes it more likely that homework gets home and gets completed. The note can be a separate sheet of paper or part of your child's assignment notebook. Basically, the child writes down her homework assignment on the home-school note and the teacher initials it to verify the assignment. The teacher also writes down a brief summary of the in-class work your child completed that day. When your child gets home, you ask for the home-school note (or homework planner) and review the homework assignments and in-class work with your child. If your child doesn't bring the note home or forgets to get it filled out, she loses all privileges for the rest of the day and must complete some "extra" homework you assign. By the way, never ask, "Do you have homework today?" Your child's answer to that question should always be "YES!" Instead, ask, "What homework do you have tonight?" or "Can I see your home-school note?"

Provide a study place that is quiet and free from distractions. Children with ADHD have a difficult time filtering out distractions while working on their homework. Many parents have their child do homework at the kitchen table. This is fine, unless the TV is on, Mom is making noise preparing supper, and big brother is talking on the phone. These activities will very easily pull your child's concentration away from schoolwork and lengthen the time it takes to finish it, creating more frustration. To solve this problem with our son, we had a desk built into his bedroom closet. There were fewer distractions and he was able to stay on task. Wherever you have your child study, reducing distractions is a big key to success.

Establish a "study hour" in your home. The study hour should be at the same time every day (remember, routines and habits!). All electronics should be turned off and everyone who is at home during that hour must study – including parents! Parents can read a book, balance the checkbook, or pay bills while the children are doing their homework. If a child completes homework before the study hour is up, she can read a book for fun. Talking is kept to a minimum, and should be focused only on topics that are being studied. If a child does not complete her homework within the hour, she should continue working on it after the hour is up. (Usually, homework can be completed in the allotted time.)

Make playing or free time contingent on completing homework. Remember the basic principle that says we do things to get something we want or get out of something we don't want? This applies to schoolwork, too. If study hour is right after school, you want your child to complete his homework then. But your child might want to play a video game. So follow the rule: "You can play your video game AFTER you finish your homework." Sometimes, parents decide children need a "break" after school and will let them play video games for a while before starting homework. This is okay if study hour is later on, after dinner. But if you want your child to do homework right after school, and you allow video game time first, it can be extremely difficult to get him to put down the game to begin homework. That's why parents should make playtime or free time contingent on completing homework.

Help your child make homework a manageable task. Sometimes, a child with ADHD will feel extremely overwhelmed by the amount of homework (no matter how much there is) on any given night. At that point, her attitude might be, "What's the use? I'll never get it all done, so why try." In this situation, telling your child to go do her homework is like telling her to go climb Mt. Everest! She sees it as an impossible task. A good strategy here is to break down the big, "impossible" task (doing homework) into several smaller, more manageable tasks. Give your child praise (and maybe a break) between each task. Eventually, the big "impossible" task will be completed!

Sibling Fighting

This is a pretty common occurrence in the animal (and human) kingdom. Siblings fight to establish dominance, test their skills, and obtain immediate reward. The result of this fighting is the development of skills necessary to survive in the world. Watching a TV special on lions in the wild, I was fascinated by how the adults in the pride allowed the young lions to spar with each other. The commentator stated that by doing so, the adults were observing their offsprings' abilities to protect and defend themselves while in the safety of the pride. Suddenly, the adult male roared and the fighters immediately stopped. Apparently, the fighting had become too rough – or the adult was simply tired of it!

Of course, among humans, yelling, hitting, and wrestling are not usually considered basic survival skills. Nevertheless, a basic drive to establish dominance does affect the behavior of our children. When one sibling has ADHD, the other siblings often become frustrated with his behaviors and, not having the advanced skills and patience of their parents, respond with verbal or physical aggression.

One day, one of my sons came to me with his fists balled up, his face red, and obvious tension throughout his body. Annoyed by the behaviors of his younger brother (who has ADHD), he spat through clenched teeth, "Dad, I know I am not supposed to fight. But if he does not get away from me RIGHT NOW, I AM GOING TO KNOCK HIS HEAD OFF!!!!" After praising him for his self-control and for not already knocking his brother's head off, I got the younger brother away from him and gave my older son time to cool down. Then I talked with him about how to handle frustrating situations such as the one that just occurred.

When you have to address sibling fighting, there are several points to keep in mind:

It is likely that both of the fighters have crossed their E-Line. That means their emotions, not their thoughts, are controlling their behaviors. Trying to discuss the situation with them may not be very effective. Ringing the bell and sending them to their respective corners to cool down may be more effective. Above all, be careful that YOU do not cross your E-Line. No matter how angry or frustrated you'd like to feel, letting your emotions dictate your behaviors will only make matters worse. Stay calm, recognizing that this is simply another opportunity for you to model for your children how to handle frustration and teach conflict resolution.

Don't try to be a referee or a judge. In the interest of "fairness," many parents make the mistake of trying to get to the bottom of who started the row, why, and who is at fault. Instead, what they hear is this:

First child: "He started it!"

Second child: "Nuh uh, HE did."

First child: "I did not, you liar."

Second child: "Yes you did! And don't call me a liar, you liar!"

This, obviously, is not going to stop until the lion (you) roars! But it takes two to fight. It doesn't really matter who started it; they are both at fault. Whoever started the fight is obviously at fault for starting it. The other one is at fault for not using appropriate conflict resolution skills and seeking help from you if those didn't work. Therefore, everyone receives consequences (a time-out or a job card).

Treat every child who is involved fairly and equally. You might be tempted to favor or side with the sibling with ADHD. Or, because this child is sometimes difficult to get along with, you may want to punish him more severely than the other sibling. Don't do either. Deliver consequences that are equal and fair. At the same time, don't let your child with ADHD off the hook because he has ADHD. Remember, he is still responsible for his behaviors. I have heard parents tell the other siblings, "You know he can't help it because of his ADHD. You should be more patient and tolerant with him." This may teach the child with ADHD that he has his parents' "sympathy" and can get away with unacceptable behaviors. It can also create resentment among the siblings, which will result in even more conflict.

Anytime there is a conflict, use it as an opportunity to have your children practice their conflict resolution skills. Once they've all calmed down below their E-Line, help them work on compromising, taking turns, sharing, etc. You may even send them to their rooms (or separate areas of the home) and have them come up with a solution before they can come back out. The room confinement may motivate them enough to work on a nonviolent solution to the problem. Be sure to praise them when they come up with a solution!

Table Manners/Eating Difficulties

Every family has different standards and expectations for mealtime. I encourage a pleasant, relaxed atmosphere with appropriate conversation. I strongly discourage any harsh words during a family dinner. The dinner table should be a pleasant time that everyone can enjoy. It is a time to reconnect with everyone in the family and discuss the joys of the day. It is not a time or place for arguing, bickering, complaining, or nagging.

If a child needs to be disciplined, take her to another room and take care of the issues, then return to the table ready to resume a pleasant conversation. Allow the child to return only after she promises to improve the mealtime environment.

Do not cater to picky eaters. The more you let your child dictate her diet, the fewer varieties of food she will eat. You spend a lot of time and energy preparing nutritious, well-balanced meals for your child. Her choice is to eat or not eat. She does not get to order something else off the menu.

Do not allow statements such as "Yuck, that's gross." If a child does not want to eat a certain food, he can say "No thank you." Any other negative statement earns a trip away from the table.

Remember, don't discipline your child at the table. Invite the child to accompany you to another room. There, you can provide whatever discipline is required. This keeps the dinner table calm, peaceful, and enjoyable for everyone else.

Bedtime and Sleep

For many children with ADHD, bedtime is one of the most difficult times of the day. If you think about it, bedtime might feel a lot like an extended time-out to your child. He is required to be isolated and stay quiet, and cannot "get out" until morning. It is no wonder most children, especially those with ADHD, have difficulty going to and staying in bed. Add to this the possible side effects of medication and your child may really struggle with bedtime.

Oftentimes, parents inadvertently make the process more difficult by responding to the child's behaviors in a rewarding manner. Again, remember the principle – we do what we do to get something we want or get out of something we don't want. It is possible that you are rewarding your child's difficult bedtime behaviors with your attention, which may be exactly what he wants.

In order to reduce the tension of bedtime, here are some suggestions to try:

Make bedtime the same time every night and follow the same routine each night. By establishing a regular bedtime, you help your child develop consistency. If bedtime is ALWAYS at 9 p.m., and you are consistent in your enforcement, there is less chance your child will try to stay up fifteen minutes later. But if bedtime fluctuates from night to night, your child may believe that behaving a certain way can get you to make it later every night. Following the same routine each night helps prepare the child for sleep and complete all necessary tasks prior to getting into bed. Your child should not have to get out of bed for a drink of water if she has already had one.

Once the routine – reading a book, saying goodnights and prayers, giving hugs and kisses – is completed, the lights go out and the day is over. You are no longer on duty. Your child is down and you have punched the time clock. What takes over is a robot that looks like you but does not speak. The robot's responsibility is to make sure your child stays in bed. The robot does not look at or talk to the child, but simply puts the child back in bed if he gets out. It will not take long for the child to learn that once you have said goodnight, he receives no more attention (except in an emergency) until morning.

Your child's bed should be used for only one thing – sleeping. This means no toys, video games, books, kites, pets, or other unnecessary baggage in bed. (I make an exception for the cuddly teddy bear that is a comfort object for the child.) If you allow your child to play in bed, then she will think bedtime is playtime, not sleep time. Make the bed a "Sleep Only" zone.

If your child continues to have extreme difficulty falling asleep, you might want to talk to your pediatrician about a possible sleep aid. Physicians often recommend the use of Melatonin to assist with sleep onset.

If your child wakes up in the middle of the night and tries to get in bed with you, take him back to his bed and tuck him back in. DO NOT SHARE YOUR BED WITH YOUR CHILDREN. This is a habit that is often very difficult to break, and it's better to just not let it get started.

Wrapping It Up

In this chapter, I've provided some suggestions for a few of the more common parenting problems involving children with ADHD. There are, of course, many other situations not covered here. However, if you practice and consistently use the basic principles of parenting, you will be able to develop strategies for resolving those other challenges.

Finally, remember that children are not one-time, two-time, or even ten-time learners. Being persistent and consistent, and realizing you have almost two decades to train your child, will help you develop patience and stick with your parenting approach as you teach and guide your child to appropriate behaviors.

Final Thoughts

I have found it helpful to remind myself that when my son was diagnosed with ADHD, it was not a "life sentence" of struggles, pain, and sorrows. Most people who have been diagnosed with ADHD grow up to have successful careers and happy lives. My son is well on his way to doing just that!

When he was younger, if I began to feel overwhelmed by the "trees," I stepped back and took a look at the entire "forest." Looking at the bigger picture helped me realize just what a blessing my son is. Sure, there were challenges. But the "bumps in the road" are what give life color. And if it hadn't been those challenges that colored our world, it likely would have been others. By meeting these challenges and successfully navigating through them, we teach our children how to navigate through their own lives as they grow and mature. Additionally, we are modeling for our children how they can best parent our future grandchildren! Now, THAT is an exciting thought!

Your child will be successful in life because you are committed to that. If you weren't, you would not have picked up this book and read it through to the end! You've decided not to treat your child as a victim, or to feel sorry for yourself, your child, and your family. You are looking for and seeing the good in your child, and are encouraging his or her best efforts.

I hope the ideas presented in this book will give you more tools to work with, and most importantly, more confidence in your abilities as you parent your child with ADHD. The strategies really do work – I know that from both research and personal experience.

As I've said several times, being a parent is a tough job, and being the parent of a child with ADHD can make it even tougher. But being the parent of any child is the most wonderful job there is! And with your help, your child can grow up to do great things!

FRANK E. BOWERS, Ph.D., is a first-time book author with the publication of *"Great Days Ahead: Parenting Children Who Have ADHD with Hope and Confidence."* Dr. Bowers and his wife Julie have three grown sons, one of whom was diagnosed with ADHD as a child.

As a Supervising Psychologist at the Boys Town Behavioral Health Clinic, Dr. Bowers counsels hundreds of children with ADHD and their families each year. A licensed psychologist, he began his work at Boys Town in 2006, where he earlier served a predoctoral internship. He also has seven years of counseling experience in private practice.

Dr. Bower earned his doctoral degree at the University of Southern Mississippi.

TARA R.S. BORSH, Psy.D, received both her master's and doctorate degrees in clinical psychology from Midwestern University in Downers Grove, Illinois. Dr. Borsh specializes in behavioral pediatrics and provides therapeutic and psychological evaluations and treatment for a wide variety of child and adolescent problems, including school difficulties, ADHD, and behavioral and emotional issues.

Dr. Borsh currently is in private practice at Chupik Counseling & Associates in central Texas. She previously was on staff at the Boys Town Behavioral Health Clinic.

Her publications include *"Teaching Social Skills to Youth with Mental Health Disorders"* and *"Improving the Social Status of Peer Rejected Youth with Disabilities."*

Index